The Passionate Lives & Leaders Series

James R. Lucas & Phil Hotsenpiller

THE PASSION PRINCIPLE:
DESIGNING A PASSIONATE
ORGANIZATION

Quintessential Books

READ BOLDLY. THINK DEEPLY. LIVE PASSIONATELY.
www.quintessentialbooks.com
BOSTON • KANSAS CITY

Copyright © 2009, Quintessential Books.

This Book Is Copyrighted Material. All Rights Are Reserved. It Is Against The Law To Make Copies Of This Material Without Getting Specific Written Permission In Advance From Quintessential Books. No Part Of This Publication May Be Reproduced, Stored In A Retrieval System, Or Transmitted In Any Form Or By Any Means, Electronic, Mechanical, Photocopying, Recording, Or Otherwise, Without Prior Written Permission Of The Publisher.

International Rights And Foreign Translation Rights Are Available Only Through Negotiation With Quintessential Books.

Printed In The United States Of America
ISBN 978-0-9823161-0-8

Cover & Layout Design by Barberhaus Design Studios
Cover Design by Jonas Barber
Layout Design by JV Kennedy

Author Photo Of James R. Lucas Copyright © 2006
By Decloud Studio. All Rights Are Reserved. Used By Permission.

Author Photo Of Phil Hotsenpiller Copyright © 2008
By Barry Morgenstein Studios. All Rights Are Reserved. Used By Permission.

Visit Quintessential Books At Http://Quintessentialbooks.Com.
For More About Passionate Lives And Leaders, Visit Http://Livesandleaders.Com.

All Trademarked Terms Are The Property Of Luman International, Inc. All Rights Are Reserved.

TABLE OF CONTENTS

Introduction: The Passionate Organization 6

Part 1: Designing a Passionate Organization 12

Part 2: Clearing the Obstacles to Building a Passionate Organization 20

Part 3: Building a Passionate Organization 36
                Rate Your Organization 42

Part 4: Forging Your Organization's Vision 44
                Answer the Big Questions 53
                Draft a Charter 65

Part 5: Investing Passionately in Your Organization's Vision 70

Time for Action 82

THE PASSIONATE ORGANIZATION

What would that cornerstone be?
There are many components of success, but only one that's not optional: ***passion***.

You can have great ideas, terrific people, plenty of money, a sound strategy – but *still* fail if there isn't enough passion to succeed. And you can be short on some of these other materials but *still* build an outstanding organization, if you have enough passion to maximize the opportunity and minimize the deficiencies. Passion is the Great Differentiator, in both individuals and in organizations.

IMAGINE THAT THERE IS A CORNERSTONE ON WHICH ALL PERFORMANCE-DRIVEN ORGANIZATIONS ARE BUILT. A CORNERSTONE THAT–IF YOU PLACED IT–WOULD ENSURE THAT YOUR TEAM OR ORGANIZATION RELENTLESSLY DELIVERED TOP-TIER RESULTS.

Imagine the difference. Suppose we have two competing organizations, each of which employs five hundred people with equal educations, experiences, talents, and skills. One organization finds a way to unleash the passionate commitment of its people—and the other does not. At Luman International, our 25 years of experience and research with hundreds of organizations tell us this: when these two organizations meet in competition, the one with passionate commitment will destroy its competitor.

This is the power of passion.

THE PASSION PRINCIPLE

Passion is **not** a mere frenzy of emotion or activity. Passion is a choice. It's a fierce commitment to adding value. It's the intense creativity summoned to achieve a worthy goal.

Passion goes far beyond commonplace ideas like "satisfaction" or "engagement"—the obsession of many organizations and the advantage of none. Passion exists at the core of meaning and purpose: Why am I working here? What are we trying to accomplish? What difference will it make? What can we do that no one else can do? What legacy can I leave behind me?

Passionate organizations have passionate people acting together toward a vision that stirs them. Passion gives people focus and drive, credibility and persuasiveness. Passion is contagious, elevating everyone's game to a much higher level.

Organizations desperately need leaders who will clear out the illusions, control, rigid structures, and pettiness that too often stand in the way of passion and commitment.

A senior leader from Boeing told us, "Passion for most organizations is a black hole. They know that they need it, know that they don't have it, and don't know how to get it." The CEO of one of the largest North American railroads admitted, "My biggest worry is that I don't know how to win the hearts and minds of our people."

Passion says, "I believe in this. I own this. I think about it even when I'm not on the clock. I know we can do this better than anyone else can. I hate mediocrity, 'good enough,' dead meetings, and the lowest common denominator. I want work to be more than a paycheck and benefits and a place to wait for weekends, vacation, and retirement. I want to be totally committed to something worth doing."

It doesn't take long to detect passion. It stands out like a rainbow in a dull gray sky.

DEFINING PASSION FOR YOURSELF

Before we get any further, take a few minutes and jot down a few sentences or key words that define the word "passion" for you.

_____

_____

_____

_____

_____

_____

HOW PREVALENT IS PASSION?

You've perhaps had the thoughts: "This organization isn't passionate. My team isn't passionate. The people around me aren't as passionate as I am."

Passion and commitment are critical for success, but we don't see much of either one in most organizations.

Think about this: in a joint survey of 755 organizations by Luman International and the American Management Association, respondents rated the levels of passion in their organization. Here's what we found:

Table 1. Passion Level by Position

Position	Passion Level
SENIOR MANAGERS	~60%
MIDDLE MANAGERS	~35%
SUPERVISORS	~25%
SKILLED PROFESSIONALS	~20%
HOURLY WORKERS	~15%

Table 1 shows the percentage of respondents who rated each level of their organization "Very High" in passion (6 or 7 on a 1-7 scale). Respondents rated only 60 percent of their *senior leaders* as highly passionate. Is it a wonder that so many organizations flounder and go out of business? How can any organization succeed if its senior leaders aren't even passionate about it?

The numbers drop off the cliff as we go deeper into the organization. The most telling point? By the time we get down to front-line workers, only 6 percent are rated as having a very high level of passion. In most organizations, this is where the mass of the people reside! This means that 94 percent of our people could take us or leave us.

In the same survey, these respondents were asked to rate the biggest drivers of high performance in their organizations. They were given an array of items to rate. Take a look at this sample of results.

Table 2. *Importance of Drivers of High Performance*

KEY FACTORS	HOW IMPORTANT IS THIS AS A POLICY FOR GETTING HIGH PERFORMANCE?	HOW WOULD YOU RATE YOUR ORGANIZATION ON DELIVERING ON THIS POLICY?
COMMITTED WORKFORCE	76.8%	37.6%
STRATEGIC PLANNING	65.0%	21.2%
REWARD/RECOGNITION	59.2%	12.8%
GOALS WITH MEASUREMENT	58.9%	17.1%
COMPENSATION/BENEFITS	50.6%	14.2%

In Table 2, the first column shows the percentage of respondents who rated each driver as "Very High" (6 or 7 on a 1-7 scale) in importance for producing a high-performance organization. Even strategic planning came in second to having a committed workforce. Over three fourths of the respondents rated a committed workforce as "Very High" in importance, while less than two thirds rated strategic planning as "Very High" in importance.

To put it bluntly, most of these respondents believe that a committed workforce is not just a nice indicator of our leadership style or our relationships with our people. A committed workforce is the difference between high performance and mediocre performance—or disaster.

How people rated their own organizations on these drivers is stunning. Just over a third scored their organizations as "Very High" on building a committed workforce. Only a fifth thought their organizations were doing a great job of strategic planning, and less than that on setting goals with measurement. The terrible numbers on two motivational standbys—reward/recognition and compensation/benefits—should finally put to rest the illusions so many have on how well these are being used. After all of the years organizations have spent building these programs, less than 15 percent of people in these 755 organizations saw their reward and recognition programs or their compensation and benefits as contributing to high performance.

The lesson is clear: Focus first on building a passionate, committed workforce. That's what this book is about.

> "OUR *ESPRIT DE CORPS* IS THE CORE OF OUR SUCCESS. THAT'S MOST DIFFICULT FOR COMPETITORS TO IMITATE. THEY CAN [BUY] ALL THE PHYSICAL THINGS. THE THING YOU CAN'T BUY IS DEDICATION, DEVOTION . . . FEELING YOU ARE PARTICIPATING IN A CAUSE OR A CRUSADE."
>
> **HERB KELLEHER, SOUTHWEST AIRLINES**[1]

"A PASSIONATE ORGANIZATION IS FOCUSED ON WHAT IT WANTS TO ACHIEVE AND DOES NOT SACRIFICE ITS PRINCIPLES AND INTEGRITY TO REACH ITS OBJECTIVES."

DAN AMSDEN, PRESIDENT, AUTOMATION ALLIANCE GROUP

DESIGNING A PASSIONATE ORGANIZATION

Rather than constantly trying to improve weaknesses and tinker with rules, leaders who want effectively passionate organizations start with proper design and solid building. They want to form organizations that will release passionate employees to deliver results.

DESIGN IT: SEVEN AREAS FOR INTENTIONAL DESIGN

Design means putting the right things in the right place in the right order. Where do we start to design an effective and highly passionate organization, an organization that graces the skyline high above its competitors?

Design Factor 1: Culture—Vision, Mission, Values, and Behaviors

A passionate organization begins with a powerful culture–a culture built around shared vision and values, mutual trust, and a strong theory of reality.

A leader's real task isn't organization design. It's *cultural* design. We're not trying to develop organizational charts and do workforce planning. We're trying to make sure we have *Passion DNA*™, a culture that unleashes passion, and a team that reduces the *need* for organizational charts and workforce planning. A Vision, Mission, Values, and Behaviors (*VMVB*™) statement answers the question of why an organization exists, what it will do to achieve success, and how the people will act and interact together along the journey. The *VMVB*™ statement is the unchanging core of an organization.

Designing around a Powerful Vision

Before retiring as chairman and CEO of Lanier Worldwide, Inc., in 2001, after a career that spanned nearly five decades, Wes Cantrell led a merger of Lanier and Ricoh, a $14 billion copier manufacturer. A world-class leader and a forward-thinking expert in marketing and sales, Cantrell also successfully acquired and integrated several companies into Lanier.

"Why in the world would racecar mechanics work faster in the race than on the shop floor?" Cantrell likes to ask. "It's because they have a very clearly defined purpose: to win a race. Working on the shop floor, the purpose is to build automobiles. People are thinking about how much they make an hour, how much time they get off, their working conditions, a bad boss. In a race, all of that goes out the window. They have one central, overriding theme, and that is to win."

The analogy provides insight into Cantrell's leadership approach. "To ignite passion in an organization and in myself, we need one central theme that's clearly defined, clear to measure, and very easy to understand when we've accomplished it. I'm more likely to be passionate with a clear vision than I am if there's something warm and fuzzy but not very clearly defined. In a business, it may be more difficult than in a sport to figure out. What is the one central thing that would ignite the passion of the organization? What is it we can really get excited about? We have to know the answers."

Cantrell recalls the moment when that question became personal. "The highlight of living my passion was when I became CEO of Lanier in 1987. We were able to put the "good name principle" into effect. I was so excited about seeing a company dedicated to the principle that a good name is more desirable than great riches. We wanted to build a company that had reputation for doing the right thing for customers and employees."

Cantrell warms to the topic. "Passion is ignited by purpose. Forget the idea of getting rich quick. It appeals to all of us to some degree or another. But it's kind of short-lived and selfish. It doesn't build a team. When you build a team around greed, sooner or later, there's going to be a lot of fallout. Instead, focus on service-led leadership."

"Always figure out who the customers are—and make them happy," Cantrell advises leaders. "On an assembly line, your customer is the person who uses your piece to build the automobile and the person who buys the automobile. Make them hilariously happy. Figure out what your boss needs to be successful. Dedicate yourself to his or her success. If your boss is successful, just by accident you'll be successful, too."

Cantrell got his first experience in customer satisfaction as a paperboy. He went to collect for the paper, and a gentleman came to the door with a handful of pennies, the 35 cents a week that Cantrell had to collect. The man just opened his hand. As the pennies scattered all over the stoop, Cantrell got down on his hands and knees, bewildered. The man said, "Now you understand how I felt when I had to pick my paper up out of the yard."

"That was a hard experience," Cantrell laughs, "but I learned how important customer service is. I spoiled my customers to the point where they expected their paper to stay nice and dry."

That kind of commitment has to come from within, Cantrell argues. "When you're really passionate about something, the idea of working long, hard hours goes out the window. You lose track of time. It's not compensation. Compensation has to be adequate; it has to be competitive. But you can't get high performance just by paying a whole lot of money. You need something that is really important to your organization and to the world—something that is much bigger than the individual. Hours become immaterial. You begin to concentrate on it and even in the middle of the night you're thinking about it. Creativity works in the subconscious of a passionate person, and you always get ideas when you're passionate about the goal."

Cantrell's passion has carried him a long way since his paper boy days. He is currently a member of the board of directors for several organizations and businesses, including Ann

Taylor Stores, Piedmont Office Realty Trust, and Southern Polytechnic State University Foundation. He received an honorary doctorate from Southern Polytechnic State University in 2002 and was named a member of the Horatio Alger Association of Distinguished Americans in 2001. Cantrell lives with his wife in Georgia and enjoys spending time with their four children and twenty-two grandchildren. With Jim Lucas, he is co-author of High-Performance Ethics: Ten Timeless Principles for Next-Generation Leadership.

We'll talk about how to put together a powerful statement of vision and values in Part 4: Forging Your Organization's Vision.

Design Factor 2: Strategy

Only after we've designed the core can we move on to designing a strategy that will achieve the organization's defined vision and mission. The majority of corporate strategies fail to achieve their original objectives, often because these strategies are not aligned with the company's culture or the changing environment. Strategy has to be flexible and dynamic. It has to prepare the organization to exploit change effectively—rather than resisting or ignoring change.

A Vision That Demands Powerful Strategy

"I am passionate about making my life matter," says Brent Martz, co-founder of Not By Sight Entertainment, LLC, a film industry production company. *"I want to be a part of a company that is focused on a vision and driven to accomplish that vision."*

Not By Sight was forged out of a passionately shared vision. When Martz met Jon Van Dyke in the spring of 2004, Van Dyke was searching for a powerful way to use his passion for filmmaking. After a series of work-related crises brought the two together for breakfast in a Los Angeles coffee shop, it soon became apparent that their combined passion for filmmaking would lead to much more.

"Jon's passion for writing and directing matched perfectly with my passion for writing and producing," Martz observes. *"Together, we maximize our strengths and depend on the other to operate in their area of passion to make our company a success."*

Martz and Van Dyke began to believe they could make a difference in the entertainment world by re-imagining family-friendly entertainment for a new generation of families.

The process started with the dream, but it took shape as the two put together a business plan and financial pro forma to attract investors. The process met with challenge after challenge. Sobered but still determined, Martz and Van Dyke found that difficulties ultimately fueled *their passion to devise a strategy that would accomplish their vision.*

"Although we are still in the start-up phase," Martz begins, "we already feel as if we are living our passion, albeit with setbacks and challenges along the way. The interesting thing is, when you're operating in your area of passion and giftedness, those challenges only fuel your fire to succeed, rather than sucking the life from you."

Just nine months after it came into being, Not By Sight Entertainment had already negotiated a two-movie contract, including worldwide distribution with the option of spinning each movie into an ongoing television series. The company's next major project has been green-lighted by Carmel Entertainment, producer of 2008's top-grossing independent film.

The company's success, says Martz, has been a direct result of the vision around which he and Van Dyke built their strategy.

Design Factor 3: Structure

Once an organization's culture and strategy are in place, it's possible to design a structure to support the organization in achieving its goals. The key question: Is this structure advancing or inhibiting our vision, mission, and strategy?

Corporate structures perform better when they possess a degree of flexibility. A flexible structure provides decision-making parameters and mechanisms for adding or creating value, rather than designating where each employee "fits into" a rigid configuration. Passionate organizations are designed more like organisms than like machines—alive, dynamic, and interconnected, rather than cog-like and cumbersome.

Design Factor 4: Process

Next, we design processes that address how individual associates and groups communicate and interact to accomplish objectives. The goal is to make process the servant rather than the master. The key question: Within our structure, will this process work to support or hinder our goals?

Designing a passionate organization means minimizing the need for policies, rules, and regulations. And we don't take the cowardly way out – designing a generic fix for a specific "person problem" – for example, issuing a policy to correct only one person's behavior rather than confronting that person and leaving everyone else alone.

Design Factor 5: People

Our culture, strategy, structure, and process must be established before we can legitimately expect people to invest and contribute at a high-performance level. Then we can make sure that our people are aligned not only with the culture but also with the specific requirements of their departments, teams, and positions.

Design Factor 6: Results

Results are the final and specific outcomes desired by the organization. They may include financial accomplishments, impact on a community, or other markers. Short of luck, we can't produce great results without designing the first five areas well.

Expected results need to be spelled out. This seems obvious, but a high percentage of working people either don't know what the required results are or think they know and are wrong. Most organizations focus way too much on roles and responsibilities and way too little on results.

Design Factor 7: Rewards

Reward and recognition programs often fail because they lack alignment with an organization's desired culture, overall direction, and strategy.

Proper alignment allows us to identify targeted, relevant rewards that support the needs of the organization. By first aligning the other six factors, effective rewards can be established based on the company's goals and its ability to fund the rewards program.

DESIGNING THE CULTURE

Take a moment to note something you would like to change in each of these areas:

Culture _____
_____
_____

Strategy _____
_____
_____

Structure _____
_____
_____

Process _____
_____
_____

People _____
_____
_____

Results _____
_____
_____

Rewards _____
_____
_____

"IT USED TO BE THE THING AROUND HERE: 'DON'T LET THE VISION STATEMENT DIE, AND DON'T LET THE VISION STATEMENT NOT BE USED.' THAT'S NOT EVEN ASKED ANYMORE. IT'S LIKE SAYING, 'DON'T USE THE WATER FOUNTAIN.' IT'S BEEN SO INTEGRATED INTO THE ORGANIZATION. IT'S WHO WE ARE, AND IT'S WHAT WE DO."

JAMES B. DESTEFANO, PRESIDENT & CEO, OCCUPATIONS, INC.

CLEARING THE OBSTACLES TO BUILDING A PASSIONATE ORGANIZATION

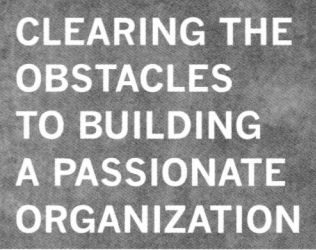

The first major step in building an extraordinary skyscraper—a passionate organization—on the site of your organization is knocking down the old, worn-out warehouses that are taking up the space. Let's take a clear-eyed look at the obstacles to building an effectively passionate organization.

AT LUMAN INTERNATIONAL, WE'VE FOUND THAT, IN ONE SENSE, ALL ORGANIZATIONS END UP BEING PASSIONATE ORGANIZATIONS.

The real question is whether they'll exhibit ***negative*** passion or ***positive*** passion. People in negatively passionate organizations are very fired up, but the fire comes out as cynicism, gossip, rumor, slander, CYA (Cover Your Assets), and all sorts of non-productive activity. If we're going to build a great organization, we have to convert those negative passions into positive ones. We need to find and build upon the locked-up positive passion of the 95 percent of our people who at core want their lives and work to count.

In doing this, we will also either marginalize the 5 percent who don't care or convert some portion of this group whose negative passion perhaps derives from derailed dreams. A key leader in one of our client organizations called himself a "recovering cynic." He had been burned but was willing to try again. When you get one of these "recovering cynics" back on the positive-passion trail, they can become a huge force for good.

Some cynics will never be reignited. But a significant percentage of them are cynics because they saw a better way but found that they couldn't live it out. They became frustrated or discouraged because they wanted to do something better with their lives and the organization and were prevented from doing it.

We try to reclaim that positive passion, but we can't beat something with nothing. We can't beat the power of negative passion by wishing it would go away, by having barbeques or Christmas parties, or by giving speeches and encouraging people to love the organization. We actually have to replace the debris of cynicism and negative passion with an effectively passionate organization. A few people may need to be replaced (especially if you've let a lot of cynics thrive), but replacing people without fixing the culture is a formula for leadership frustration and a guarantee of cultural weakness.

There are five large obstacles to building a passionate organization. All five have to be cleared before a passionate organization can rise from the debris.

LET'S CONSIDER HOW TO CLEAR THESE OBSTACLES.

Obstacle 1: Myths and Illusions

FIVE OBSTACLES TO BUILDING A PASSIONATE ORGANIZATION:
> MYTHS AND ILLUSIONS
Exhaustion and disengagement
An oppressive culture
Misalignment
Core substitution

Morris Dickstein said, "[The world] is always at the edge of falsehood."[2] This important point is more fully addressed in ***The Reality Principle: Exploiting Change and Crisis with Courage and Passion,*** the seventh title in the PASSIONATE LIVES & LEADERS series. Here, we simply want to point out that the first major obstacle to building a passionate organization is a belief in myths and illusions–falsehoods about organizations and leadership.

Myths

The foundational problem is a belief in "management" of people. This myth says, "I can get the best performance out of people by controlling, directing, and monitoring them. I can succeed by building elaborate performance management and forced-ranking systems in which people are treated as components of a machine that can be evaluated, replaced, and removed from the system when they're worn out."

This belief is a myth, the Myth of Management. Why? In the first place, it's useless to try to manage anyone else. Very few people will allow themselves to be managed or controlled. They may pretend to collaborate, but inside, their resistance remains strong and leaves no room for passion and commitment. Leaders need to give up on this myth.

In fact, even if people allowed themselves to be controlled, leaders wouldn't know how to do it effectively. The elaborately detailed Five Year Plans of the old Soviet Union were devised by experts and backed up by tyranny, and they were spectacular failures. Trying to manage others is a very tricky business. Most of us have enough trouble trying to manage ourselves.

When we give up this myth, we open ourselves up to true leadership and the possibility of igniting widespread passion. There's a huge difference between management and leadership. Here's the contrast:

MANAGEMENT	VS.	LEADERSHIP
CONTROLLING		RELEASING
DIRECTING		RESPECTING
MONITORING		TRUSTING
RANKING		AGREEING
SUPERVISING		INSPIRING

Management does have a role, just not with people. Great leaders apply management to processes and systems, and they apply leadership to people. They don't use their tools on the wrong tasks.

Great leaders know that managing people is more likely to stifle growth than to enhance it. In fact, the word "management" comes from a Latin root word which means "hands on." The related word "bureaucracy" means "the rule of the desk" or "the rule of the office." These are not good approaches for leading human beings—unless leaders want to turn their people into "pay-for-pulse" employees who use their creativity to avoid responsibility and shift blame.

The management hierarchy can't be "tweaked" or "adjusted" to produce a passionate organization. The chain-of-command can't be reformed. We have to break the chain to set our people free. We have to cut through it directly by reducing and eliminating any unnecessary policies, procedures, and rules. The real question: "Are these rules our servants or our masters?" Rules are great as tools but disasters as masters.

Great leaders move beyond hierarchical thinking, not by eliminating positions of authority or distinct roles and responsibilities in the organization, but by taking these actions:

- *Inviting others to embrace a new way of leading.* It's a hard thing to change a leadership style—but not as hard as using a bad one.
- *Creating new teams or business units or divisions with these fresh approaches toward leading people and managing things.* Sometimes it's easier to avoid the clutter and build something new from the ground up.
- *Involving others in setting and achieving important goals.* When we're thinking clearly, we know how much we don't know and how much more others can help us know.

- *Using planning to guide change in the culture rather than to defend the culture that already exists.* Most organizations develop expertise in modifying the inconsequential.

> **"PROBLEMS CANNOT BE SOLVED AT THE SAME LEVEL OF AWARENESS THAT CREATED THEM."**
> **ALBERT EINSTEIN, PHYSICIST[3]**

- *Re-educating ourselves and our leaders to adjust our leadership style.* We can't do things the same, stale way and get a different, fresh result. Superior cultural change and superior leadership development are two mutually reinforcing powers.

Illusions

What are illusions? The book *Fatal Illusions* gives this description: "Illusions are living things. Like layer upon layer of paint added to a rotting wall, illusions tend to produce more illusions. They cause us to 'solve' a problem by adding another layer of illusion, and, when the rot breaks through, to paint it again."[4]

At Luman International, we often find in our client organizations that one or more of the 12 *Fatal Illusions*™ have taken hold and developed a pervasive influence. Some will kill your organization more quickly than others. Some illusions cause a long, slow death, while some destroy an organization quickly. The more illusions the organization holds, the faster and more devastating the deterioration will be.

Some *Fatal Illusions*™[1]
- "Having a mission statement means we know who we are."
- "Of course our people understand what's important."
- "Just give people a chance and they'll work together."
- "We don't need passion if we have a good plan."

---

[1] *For more on the devastating illusions that have been shown to destroy organizations--and solutions that address these unrealities, see* Fatal Illusions: Shredding a Dozen Unrealities that Can Keep Your Organization from Success *(Kansas City: Quintessential Books, 2001).*

Once a *Fatal Illusion*™ has gotten into the cultural DNA, no one is able to talk safely about its existence. Evidence to the contrary–like the fact that people are working on unimportant things–is systematically suppressed. Often, the illusion itself is defended. It's often supported from the top, because it has become the organization's mental model, the way people think about things. Its power can be difficult to break, unless someone actually decides to attack it.

"ORGANIZATIONS HAVE DEVELOPED A FUNCTIONAL BLINDNESS TO THEIR OWN DEFECTS. THEY ARE NOT SUFFERING BECAUSE THEY CANNOT RESOLVE THEIR PROBLEMS, BUT BECAUSE THEY CANNOT SEE THEIR PROBLEMS." JOHN GARDNER, WRITER[5]

Sooner or later, we have to get past the notion, the *fatal* notion, that "perception is reality." Perception is *not* reality. **Reality** is reality. People will act on their perceptions as though they are reality, but that fact doesn't make them real. The more deeply people embrace erroneous perceptions, the more they become reality-impaired.

The worst scenario is when the illusion is so firmly embedded that there's a passion around protecting it. Passion can be used in harmful ways, most of which begin with ignoring truth and embracing illusions.

"BELIEF IN TRUTH BEGINS WITH DOUBTING ALL THAT HAS HITHERTO BEEN BELIEVED TO BE TRUE." FRIEDRICH NIETZSCHE, PHILOSOPHER[6]

If we're going to build a passionate organization different from most on the planet, we're going to have to doubt some things. We're going to have to doubt the things that need to be doubted. We need to challenge our illusions so that we can begin to embrace reality.

Illusions have to be shredded so that we can finally see our problems. Only when we align with reality can we begin to change it effectively.

Obstacle 2: *Exhaustion and Disengagement*

FIVE OBSTACLES TO BUILDING A PASSIONATE ORGANIZATION:
Myths and illusions
> **EXHAUSTION AND DISENGAGEMENT**
An oppressive culture
Misalignment
Core substitution

Over a long period of time, if people have been misused or not allowed to invest themselves in the organization, they simply check out.

Unfortunately, they sometimes check out without actually leaving. There are way too many people who have already retired but then stay on the job and continue to take a paycheck.

We have to ask ourselves, are we allowing enough time for rest and renewal? Are we allowing people time to think? It's ironic that we live in a "knowledge economy" where no one ever has the time to think. Media and technology and instant access have, inch-by-inch, stolen our ability to reflect.

Great leaders create space for their people to rest and think and create so they don't become stressed. And they allow people to volunteer to work on different projects and in different areas so that their energy and passion can be renewed and so they don't become bored. Performance drops off precipitously when people become either stressed or bored. It looks like this:

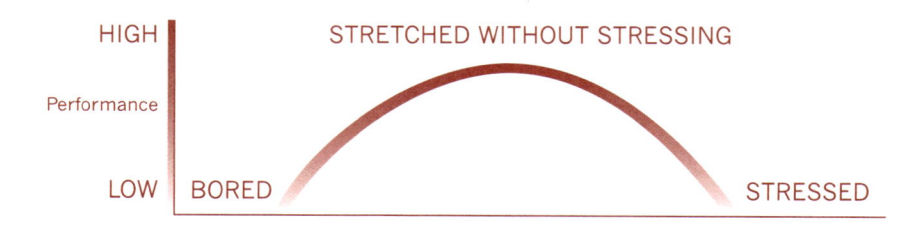

<chart showing inverted U-curve: HIGH Performance at top, LOW at bottom; BORED on left, STRESSED on right; peak labeled "STRETCHED WITHOUT STRESSING">

Leaders who build passion find a way to manage both the stress and boredom levels in their organizations. They stretch their people without stressing them.

Based on the Yerkes-Dodson Curve; see Matthews, Gerald, D. Roy Davies, and Stephen J. Westerman. Human Performance. New York: Psychology Press, 2000.

Are we allowing people an opportunity to innovate, to use imagination, to tap into the creative nature that's at the core of being human? Are they able to act on those ideas that Gifford Pinchot calls *intrapreneuring*?

Burnout is often discussed, but here's the bottom line: It doesn't come from working hard. Look at some organizations where people work incredibly long hours and seem refreshed at the end of the week. Should this fact make us pause and wonder if something else is driving the burnout around us?

"PASSION CREATES OWNERSHIP, AND PEOPLE PUT MORE OF THEMSELVES INTO ANY ACTIVITY THAT THEY TAKE OWNERSHIP IN."

DAN AMSDEN, PRESIDENT, AUTOMATION ALLIANCE GROUP

Obstacle 3: An Oppressive Culture

FIVE OBSTACLES TO BUILDING A PASSIONATE ORGANIZATION:
Myths and illusions
Exhaustion and disengagement
> **AN OPPRESSIVE CULTURE**
Misalignment
Core substitution

The next obstacle to building a passionate organization is a tyrannical culture. Oppressive cultures are usually not constructed by design but grow over time through a buildup of bad practices and bad ideas. Often they start out with someone's good intentions to correct a problem or to reform a problem person.

In domineering cultures, enthusiastic voices are drowned out rather than welcomed. There's no place for mavericks or maverick thinking. Dissent is not considered a way to improve ideas but a way to create disharmony. Spontaneity puts people outside the system, making them "rule-breakers" rather than heroes trying to make things better.

Oppressive cultures tend to build layer upon layer of bureaucracy, layer upon layer of management, with intertwined layers of rules and regulations. Leaders in these cultures see the negative passions in their organizations and blame them on bad people rather than bad practice.

At times, instead of trying to design an alternative, the leaders manipulate these passions for personal ends. For example, they put out rumors through the grapevine, hoping to influence the organization with "their" material. (The grapevine, of course, has a life of its own and tends to spread its own inaccuracies regardless of management's efforts). In oppressive cultures, the grapevine is the primary source of people's knowledge and information, however inaccurate or exaggerated it might be, because no one trusts the people at the top.

In harsh cultures, the wrong people are often promoted or lifted up as examples. The person who is crushing morale but got slightly better results in the last quarter is lifted up as a paragon, while the organization sidelines the leader who is trying to build a team that's effective over many years and in many areas. Oppressive cultures are callous to people's feelings, often the primary drivers of human action.

However much anger and rage and indignation exist in an oppressive culture, over time the futility lulls everyone to sleep. People end up sleepwalking through their days and waiting to go home while the organization sails in a leisurely manner toward the iceberg.

DE-EVOLUTION OF CORPORATE CULTURE

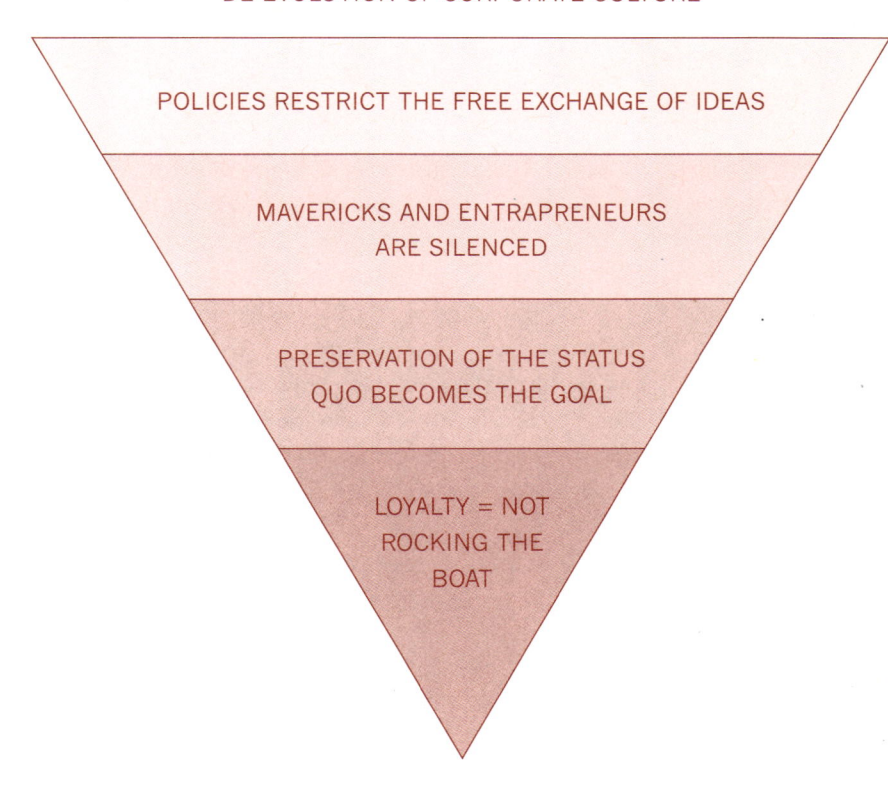

- POLICIES RESTRICT THE FREE EXCHANGE OF IDEAS
- MAVERICKS AND ENTRAPRENEURS ARE SILENCED
- PRESERVATION OF THE STATUS QUO BECOMES THE GOAL
- LOYALTY = NOT ROCKING THE BOAT

The Result:
An Oppressive Culture that Kills Passion and Creativity

Obstacle 4: Misalignment

FIVE OBSTACLES TO BUILDING A PASSIONATE ORGANIZATION:
Myths and illusions
Exhaustion and disengagement
An oppressive culture
> **MISALIGNMENT**
Core substitution

Even if we have good people with high personal energy levels who want to commit to excellence, they still need to know what the commitment means. In too many organizations, there is a gross misalignment between each person's individual passions, goals, and competencies and what the organization needs or expects.

This misalignment could come from an organization-wide absence of a clear vision, mission, values, or defined behaviors, or from an unclear line of sight between these factors and the individual—or both. Maybe the organization is working in areas outside the *Core Excellencies*™ and passions of its people. Perhaps we have a mismatch between people and the organization, their department, their boss, or their position. Or maybe there are overlapping responsibilities because we haven't clearly differentiated two jobs.

Like someone driving a car that hasn't been aligned in many years down a highway at 100 miles per hour, we're headed for an accident if the organization and its people are seriously misaligned.

Staying in Alignment over Time

People call from around the globe to talk to Mike Vietro.

They call to talk about cars, about art, about watches—but mostly, they call to talk about vintage Corvettes.

Vietro is the founder of Corvette Mike's, a company that for more than 30 years has specialized in finding and placing rare Corvettes.

When people call him, they're looking for a specific car, and usually one that's nearly impossible to find. Combing through thousands of records he has collected over decades, though, he typically finds it there in his database—or by calling around to "the guys" in the know or to someone referred by the guys.

"We're talking about rare collectibles," Vietro explains. "In the universe of Corvettes,

because of racing heritage, the horsepower of the engine, and the combination of the engine and the options, people want a very specific car. They want the patina; they want the original paint, the original carpets, the original steering wheel, the original battery—if they can get it—from the '60s! Where do you find something like that? I find them. I know where they are."

Most importantly, they also want the factory original documents that accompanied the car as it left the factory. Vietro finds those, too.

Through the years, plenty of people have suggested that Vietro reinvent himself: "You know, you've got a good name in the business. Why don't you get into four-wheel drive trucks? Why don't you mix it and do the old Datsun 240Zs? Maybe you should think about doing a little bit more in the muscle cars."

But Vietro has kept his focus despite other opportunities. "I've tried it; I've done fairly well," Vietro responds to his would-be advisers. But he also admits that he has gotten to the point in his life where if it's not fun and enjoyable, it's just not worth doing.

"I have finally gotten to a place that makes dollars and sense within myself. So why mess with a good thing? As much as I appreciate those cars and like to hear about originality in those cars," says Vietro, "they just don't thrill me like the hunt of the Corvette. Part of the passion that I can actually revel in is the hunt. And part of it is staying on my own clear path."

"YOU HAVE TO HAVE PASSION TO GET RESULTS. YOU CAN'T OPERATE WITHOUT IT—ABSOLUTELY NOT."

DAVID GREEN, FOUNDER, PRESIDENT & CEO, HOBBY LOBBY STORES

Obstacle 5: Core Substitution

FIVE OBSTACLES TO BUILDING A PASSIONATE ORGANIZATION:
Myths and illusions
Exhaustion and disengagement
An oppressive culture
Misalignment
> CORE SUBSTITUTION

What if your organization is actively involved in trying to ignite passion but nothing seems to work? It's possible that the cornerstone of the organization is missing–the strong cultural core we discussed in Part 1: Designing a Passionate Organization. The cultural core tells an organization why it exists, where it's going, what everyone will do to achieve success, how people will act and interact along the way, and how they will set goals and establish plans that will allow them to live the vision.

Organizations that don't have this strong cultural core tend to start a fruitless process of substitution:

- For example, if we don't establish the cultural core, we might first substitute strategic planning. We think, "We'll come up with some strategies and tactics, and that will become our core. That will identify us." The strategy fails virtually every time because the strategy isn't connected to the bigger picture and because it also has to serve as a substitute for the cultural core. When the strategy doesn't work, we try another strategy. Then that doesn't work, so we try another and another and another. Finally, in frustration, we give up and look for something else to fill the hole.

- The next thing we might try is structural change. We say, "Let's reorganize. Let's move people around. Let's revise the organization chart. Let's try Jessica and Luis over here and Toby and Kiana over there and see if that works." After we try a series of reorganizations (and it's not too hard to think of many organizations in the last 10 years that have gone through multiple, sometimes annual, reorganizations), we find that the reorganization fails. Once again, we're reorganizing but we don't know why we exist, where we're going, or how we're going to get there. We're making new charts, but we're not making progress.

- Structure failing, we look to process. "Maybe the problem is that our processes just don't work," we imagine. We embrace the process solution *du jour*, whether it's business process reengineering, Total Quality Management, Six Sigma, or supply-chain management. Now we have a new process, and we think this is going to be our salvation. But our attempt to substitute a process for the missing core (predictably) doesn't work. Small improvements but no breakthrough: for example, we really need large-scale innovation, but now we're fenced in by Six Sigma. Once again we're trying to fill a vacuum with the wrong things – good things in their own right, but bad things as substitutes.

- Next, we take a look at our people: "Nothing seems to be working. We don't know why we're here, where we're going, what we're going to do to get there, how we should go about things, how we should organize to get the job done, or what kinds of processes will really work, but there is a problem somewhere. The problem must be the people." We start looking into changing people: "Let's fire these people; let's educate these people; let's do *something* with these people, because people are the problem." We try changing the people, and we still don't improve our results. In his 60 years of experience, quality expert Edwards Deming observed, problems were caused by the system and not by the people 85 percent of the time.

- Other things failing, we might look at changing the reward structure. "Maybe we just need to give them more money. Maybe we need to change the way we compensate people. Maybe we need to find some recognition programs and motivational schemes that will get people fired up to do the job." But these approaches have a very short-term effect, and then we're back to where we were before we started. The whole problem: we're trying to get the arms and legs moving before we get the heart of the organization beating.

An organization riddled with myths and illusions, exhaustion and disengagement, oppression, misalignment, and core substitution—any or all of the above—is an organization designed to be mediocre in the long term both in its form and in its function.

And very short on passion.

CLEARING THE OBSTACLES

Identify which of the five enemies of a passionate organization presents the biggest threat to your organization.

Myths & Illusions   Exhaustion & Disengagement   Oppressive Culture

Misalignment   Core Substitution

Now jot down a preliminary plan for clearing that obstacle in your own sphere of influence first. For example, if misalignment is rampant in your organization, draw up a chart connecting your position and responsibilities to the overall vision and success of the organization (as you see them). If the culture is oppressive, write down some ways to improve the situation in your area without jeopardizing your career.

_____
_____
_____
_____
_____
_____
_____
_____
_____
_____
_____
_____
_____
_____
_____
_____

> "ONE OF THE THINGS THAT IS EXTREMELY IMPORTANT IS THAT PEOPLE UNDERSTAND THEIR ROLES AND HOW THEY CAN MAKE A DIFFERENCE."
>
> DAN COLE, SENIOR VP, ADMINISTRATION, AMEREN ENERGY, FUELS, & SERVICES

BUILDING A PASSIONATE ORGANIZATION

Build It: 10 Keys to Building a Passionate Organization™

3

NOW THAT OUR DESIGN IS IN PLACE AND THE OBSTACLES AND DEBRIS ARE CLEARED, WE CAN BEGIN BUILDING.

Because every industry, every organization, and every group of people will be different, each building process will have unique features. There are, however, 10 Keys to building a passionate organization—10 Keys identified by Luman International's quarter-century of work with hundreds of organizations. Here they are:

Key 1: Truth

When leaders fail to face reality, align with it, and tell the truth, they create an information vacuum that *will* be filled – by comfortable but fatal illusions, by rumors, by whatever dark gossip the grapevine can generate. In this kind of truth-starved environment, passion cannot flourish. A leader who wants to cultivate passion must first embrace truth—and structure ways to get truth spoken everywhere in the organization.

> ### *Building on Truth*
>
> *After a senior partner acted with questionable integrity, David Jack's firm had to act quickly to save its reputation—and its clients.*
>
> *In fact, the clients themselves sounded the early alarm. When some of the largest ones announced they were leaving the firm, Jack and the other partners went into action to find out what had happened. After a detailed examination revealed problematic behavior by a senior partner, they decided to sever ties with this partner immediately to secure the clients' trust.*
>
> *The move was disruptive and costly, but the firm's character remained intact.*
>
> *"That is the base upon which good relationships are built, and we couldn't compromise it," Jack says. "We instilled confidence in clients because we believed with conviction that our process was sound: we knew we were doing the right thing."*
>
> *Temporary failure wasn't fatal. Taking as their motto a line by Roman poet Virgil— "They can conquer who believe they can"—the remaining partners focused on long-term performance. The firm came through the crisis stronger than ever, says Jack, who has since left and now serves as Senior Vice President of Investment at UBS Financial Services.*
>
> *"The clients that grasped the integrity issue came back to us. Those that didn't we were better off without."*

Key 2: Alignment

Too often, leaders believe they can get people to work together and perform by introducing policies, procedures, reporting, job descriptions, and evaluations. But remember, although we can *manage things* (processes, systems, programs, initiatives), we can only *lead people*. This reality means that we have to create alignment rather than rely on control. Passionate organizations are built around a powerful shared vision, a conception of who we are and who we want to be, and mutual purpose and values. Rather than substituting other things for this core, define it and then align the organization around it.

Key 3: Involvement

Michael Winner once humorously defined a team as "a lot of people doing what I say." We may cloak this type of monarchy in terms like *empowerment*—"I'm the king or queen with all of the power, but I will condescend to share a little with you"—but we cannot and should not expect positive passion to flourish under a dictatorship. The alternative, *powersharing*™, means we invite people to invest their powers—their passion capital, their thinking capital, and their determination—in a shared vision.

Key 4: Risk

Our people are not *costs* or *resources* or *assets*. They are *investors*. If we want a passionate organization, we have to reward the risk they are taking when they invest their time and effort and experience and creativity. Raising the *ROHI*™—*the Return on Human Investment*™—means getting the maximum return for the individual, for the team, and for the organization. To make this happen, we need to allow people to take risks and to make *intelligent mistakes*™ in pursuit of the vision, strategy, and goals.

Key 5: Innovation

Leadership means creating a safe place for dangerous change. Great organizations don't try to survive change or even thrive during change, but rather try to *exploit* change. Passionate organizations flourish in an environment that expects innovation from every person at every level. They focus on making customers' and partners' experiences better. Passionate organizations give people time to think, provide some structure (but not too much), measure innovation, and reward and recognize it fully. (For more on innovation, see ***The Thinking Principle: Using Passion to Innovate and Create Value,*** the third title in the PASSIONATE LIVES AND LEADERS SERIES).

Key 6: Possibility

Great leaders focus their organizations on possibilities rather than limitations, results rather than methods, and freedom rather than controls. Passionate organizations are engaged in building the future rather than defending or lamenting the past. We have to paint a positive, powerful picture of the future because people will commit to an idea or dream or goal or cause as it is embodied in an organization. The *cause*—not the *organization*—is what inspires passion.

Key 7: Challenge

Living out a noble vision to serve human beings is a worthy challenge for our organizations. Once we set our sights on serving the customer or client and involving our organizations in positive action, our people can invest their passion in things that matter. We need to give our people "stretch goals" to sustain their growth, extend their capabilities, and fuel their passion. When we have people who are passionate about that goal, they may have differing ideas about how to carry it out. We need to make sure people know that it's safe–and *expected*–to disagree respectfully and intelligently rather than sinking into "groupthink" or cowardly silence.

Key 8: Teaching

Knowledge is power for an organization – but only when it is *shared*, not when it is *hoarded*. We are trying to develop a community of rugged individuals freely cooperating, freely sharing, freely teaching. This can only happen when we provide enough of the right kind of information and develop the right kind of skills so that people can improve processes and add value.

Key 9: Communication

Communication that encourages passion is honest, open, lavish, enthusiastic, and seamless: everyone gets the same message, even if the level of detail is different. To build passionate organizations, we get data, wisdom, expectations, and feedback flowing down. We get ideas, innovations, problems, mistakes, and bad news flowing up. We get good thinking and practices flowing horizontally through the organization. And we get knowledge and wisdom flowing to the new value-creation "hot spots" in the organization, even if that stream can't be easily diagrammed.

Key 10: Trust

Leaders tend to cling to the myth that loyalty is the hallmark of a workforce. But effective organizations don't need *loyalty* to a person or creed; they need *commitment* to a worthy, shared vision and values. Journeying together toward a common destination fosters trust, and that hard-earned trust creates passion—both for the journey and for the success of those who are sharing it with us.

"YOU CAN FEEL IT IN THE AIR. FROM THE RECEPTIONIST TO THE CEO, THERE IS A FEELING OF PURPOSE IN A PASSIONATE ORGANIZATION. PEOPLE ARE WORKING NOT FOR MONEY OR FOR THE BOSS, BUT BECAUSE THEY ARE TRULY EXCITED ABOUT THEIR CONTRIBUTION TO A GREATER PURPOSE."

KURT MCCASLIN, PRESIDENT AND GENERAL MANAGER, ANADARKO (BRAZIL)

"PASSION AND COMMITMENT ARE TOTALLY ESSENTIAL TO PERFORMANCE. WITHOUT PASSION, YOU HAVE EMPLOYEES WHO ARE JUST PUTTING IN TIME."

DAVID GREEN, FOUNDER, PRESIDENT & CEO, HOBBY LOBBY

"TALK ABOUT A LACK OF PASSION, A LACK OF COMMITMENT - IT COMES FROM THE FACT THAT MOST COMPANIES DO NOT LOOK ON PEOPLE AS REAL, IMPORTANT CONTRIBUTORS THAT ARE GOING TO BE THERE LONG-TERM."

FRED KOCHER, PRESIDENT & GENERAL MANAGER (RETIRED),
AAR CORPORATION

RATE YOUR ORGANIZATION

On a scale of 1 to 10, rate your organization on each of the keys. A rating of 1 means there is no evidence of this key in your organization and 10 means your organization exemplifies the key trait.

Truth	1	2	3	4	5	6	7	8	9	10
Alignment	1	2	3	4	5	6	7	8	9	10
Involvement	1	2	3	4	5	6	7	8	9	10
Risk	1	2	3	4	5	6	7	8	9	10
Innovation	1	2	3	4	5	6	7	8	9	10
Possibility	1	2	3	4	5	6	7	8	9	10
Challenge	1	2	3	4	5	6	7	8	9	10
Teaching	1	2	3	4	5	6	7	8	9	10
Communication	1	2	3	4	5	6	7	8	9	10
Trust	1	2	3	4	5	6	7	8	9	10

Total Score_____

Think of your organization's score as its grade for the term. A score of 90 percent or better is an "A." Below 60 percent is a failing mark.

Now, jot down why you assigned each score and what could be done to improve it.

Truth _____

Alignment _____

Involvement _____

Risk _____

Innovation _____

Possibility _____

Challenge _____

Teaching _____

Communication _____

Trust _____

Take your 2 or 3 lowest scores and meet with your team to brainstorm ways to improve them. Get an outside facilitator to help if necessary. The goal is to build a passionate organization by design, from the inside out, so sustainable success will be yours.

FORGING YOUR ORGANIZATION'S VISION

The Roman statesman Seneca observed, "If one doesn't know to which port one is sailing, no wind is favorable."[7] If people know where we're going, they can align with the vision, commit to it, support it, enhance it, and even determine whether we achieve it. And yet, astonishingly, 95 percent of employers don't even tell their people what the strategy is![8] How can people help us get to our destination if they don't know what it is?

IN A RECENT SURVEY,[9] TWO OF THE TOP THREE THINGS THAT PEOPLE WANTED THEIR EMPLOYERS TO DO WERE "SHOW HOW TO FIT INTO THE COMPANY'S VISION" AND "EXPLAIN THE COMPANY'S VISION."

The core problem in most organizations? They *have* no clear vision, no clear purpose, no clear direction. This lack of identity creates little motivation among the people who are already there and offers nothing to lure new people.

Pulled in Two Directions: The Vacuum of a Missing Vision

You might not guess the challenge that recently confronted one of the longest-active corporations in California. But Dr. Jeff Decker saw that challenge firsthand.

"They were trying to make a transformation that put real demands on them," says Decker, professor and chair of the Master of Arts in Organizational Leadership at Biola University.

The company traces its history back to 1849, when the founder sold tools to miners during the California Gold Rush. Today, it is mainly an aerospace manufacturing company.

"The existing business is very mature, very stable," says Decker. "They bought a company of 250 research rocket scientists in Alabama. They were trying to bring together two completely different business realities, which you might think of as the perfect storm. You have two different businesses. You have a large geographical distance between the two companies. You also had a significant style difference in the management. The combination of those factors led to an incredibly 'interesting' organizational situation."

When Decker first met with the president and two senior vice presidents of the business that was acquired, they had a two-hour discussion. The executives piled all the frustrations of their first nine months together on Decker. Decker calls it an "organizational exorcism." But where other people saw dead ends, he saw possibilities.

"My passion is to find places where people are struggling and willing to learn," says Decker. To thrive in a new millennium, he points out, this old-school, space-age company had to learn to forge a common vision.

A lack of vision is a special problem for capturing younger Baby Boomers, Gen-Xers, and Millennials who want their lives to be organically connected to something powerful, to work for something greater than themselves.

Sometimes the organization itself isn't even big enough to contain their expectations. They want the organization to transcend the market and take positive social action. More and more, workers are approaching life holistically, believing, "I can be passionate about this job if I know that I'm making a difference in the world." To resonate with these emerging leaders, organizational life today has to fill their desire to leave a legacy, *even if they are only there a short time*. The organizations that can provide that opportunity will consistently attract the most passionate, highest-performing people.

To build this kind of organization, we have to know where we're going, both as individuals and together. We need to make sure that our paths and the organization's path are not just running parallel but merging. Leaders who want to build great teams or organizations need a clear vision forged *by* the people who are already a passionate, committed part of the organization. Drawing all of their ideas, personalities, and passions into the process will build something unique that's guaranteed to draw other like-minded people like a beacon.

In short, we need to *forge a shared vision.*

Forge – Vision is not something you can find by going to a mountain by yourself. You can't slap it together over dinner and drinks with the senior leadership team. We have to fashion vision out of the best of what our organizations already are and the best of what we want them to be. Together, we have to wrestle with the questions, "What already exists here that is good? How do we make the good even better by melding it with the best of what we can become?"

Shared – If vision is only owned by senior management or by 5 or 10 percent of the people in an organization, a lot of gold nuggets of insight remain on the ground, along with almost all of the potential commitment. Great leaders understand that they have to *involve* people to get *Be-In*™ – rather than *sell* a vision to get "buy-in" (the traditional approach). There has to be mutual agreement about the destination and the path.

Vision – Vision doesn't mean a fuzzy statement announcing, "We'd like everyone to know that we're the best thing that ever happened." An actionable vision is very clear and very specific. It explains why we're here and where we want to go as a team or organization.

"OUR COMPANY WENT FROM FOURTH QUARTILE TO FIRST QUARTILE IN A SHORT TIME AFTER IMPLEMENTING YOUR VMVB™ PROCESS…. QUITE SIMPLY, WE FINALLY FOCUSED THE BUSINESS ON DOING THE THINGS WE WERE TRULY GOOD AT— INSTEAD OF FOCUSING ON THE THINGS WE WISHED WE WERE GOOD AT."

SENIOR VICE PRESIDENT, A GLOBAL ENERGY COMPANY

There are four major phases in forging a shared vision. Complete them to draw people toward it and toward each other.

Phase 1: Preparing the Troops

THE FOUR PHASES OF FORGING A SHARED VISION:
> PREPARING THE TROOPS
  Starting the revolution
  Stirring the revolution
  Keeping the revolution alive

The first task for a leader who wants to forge a shared vision is to heat the forge—to prepare the organization for a dynamic process that will result in a shared vision. What does that require? Here are five important rules to keep in mind.

Rule 1: Differentiate Between the 95 and the 5

Most organizations are built to restrain and control the people who habitually act in ways contrary to the organization's best interest – the "5 percenters." Instead, we have to build our organizations around the 95 percent of our people who really want their work lives to count for something, even if they feel that they don't count right now. This is the *Rule of the 95 and the 5*™.

We're always going to have a few bad apples. But we want to build our organizations around the *best* 95 percent and what they would like to do, not around the 5 percent who don't want to do anything useful or be part of anything meaningful. Don't build an organization around policies, procedures, rules, or regulations in an attempt to control a handful of obnoxious people. They'll get around whatever system you design anyway, and you're going to squelch the life out of the 95 in the meantime.

Always focus on the 95. What are the "better angels of our nature"? What are the better angels of *their* natures? How do we access those qualities?

Rule 2: Remember that You Can't Beat Something with Nothing

We can't bring the passion of the 95 percent to life just by imitating sports coaches and giving rah-rah speeches. A powerful force of lethargy and inertia reigns in most organizations. We're not going to move the massive block of an organization more than an inch with motivational talks that remain disconnected from reality. It takes a lot of force to get that much mass moving in a new direction. But the alternative is lumbering along as an organization, glacier-like, for years or decades, doomed to mediocrity or disappearance.

Vision is alluring and integrative, while opinion is distracting and fragmenting. Vision is more powerful than opinion, and its influence is stronger than the power of the grapevine. If you don't have a powerful, shared vision, the void will always be filled with conflicting opinions about what you should do. And while opinion tends to be dogmatic and personal, vision is expansive, imaginative, attractive, and (if we do it right) shared.

Rule 3: Avoid Dooming the Organization to Mediocrity

Howard Schultz, the founder and CEO of Starbucks, said, "A company is doomed to mediocrity unless it has passionate staff who believe in its values and its message."[10] Mediocrity always creeps in when passion is absent. Starbucks built its success by remembering the vision principle. Organizations that forget it develop run-of-the-mill performance and second-rate attitudes. Their people wait for Fridays, vacations, and retirement. They hire people by offering a lot of money, but they have nothing of real substance to attract anyone who is passionate. Mediocrity is a terrible place for any organization to be, but that's the destiny of all organizations without vision.

Rule 4: Answer the Big Questions Well

We have to answer the Big Questions. With everyone—leaders in our organizations, members of teams, new people coming in—we should ask the Big Questions and then listen for answers.

Several years ago, I was on a panel at Northwestern University's Kellogg

School of Business with senior executives from Target, McDonald's, and Booz Allen. Someone asked, "How do you know when it's time to make a major transformational change?" The answers of the others on the panel were insightful and valuable. Here's what I said: "Regardless of your current level of success, you know it's time to make a change *when the leaders and others in your organization can no longer answer 5 big questions well.*"

Here are the questions:
- *Why are we here? (a vision question)*
- *Where are we going? (a second vision question)*
- *What are we going to do to make it to this destination? (a mission question)*
- *How are we going to act and interact in order to reach our destination? (a values question)*
- *How are we going to set goals and objectives and establish tactics that will allow us to arrive successfully? (a strategy question)*

Why Are We Here?

What's our purpose for being? If we weren't here, would it make any difference to anyone? A lot of people talk about "branding" and "value propositions," but those might end up being superficial or short-lived if they aren't tied to some worthy purpose. Unless we can give a concise answer to this question, we aren't in the race for top-tier results.

Where Are We Going?

If we're providing products and services but we don't know why "us" rather than "them," we don't have any map to guide the organization. If we only want more sales and revenues, we've fallen into the trap of growth for growth's sake—and it can too easily become a cancerous growth.

What Are We Going to Do to Make It to This Destination?

Once we know why we're here and where we're going, what are we willing to do to get there? What are our *critical success factors*? What are the real drivers that are going to take us to our hoped-for destination?

Most organizations just set goals: "We'd like to have our sales (or revenues) go up by X percent in the next year," or "We'd like to have X percent more market share in the next year." But these goals don't define for actual human beings the things they can do to help achieve those goals. Having a clear and specific way to contribute to an important vision drives passion. Your people need to be able to say, "I see where we're going. I see what I can do to get from here to there. I know what our critical success factors are, and I know what they are right down to my department level, my team level, my individual level." When that happens, we have an engine with more power than we might have imagined possible.

How Are We Going to Act and Interact in Order to Reach Our Destination?

What kinds of values and behaviors are going to contribute to the powerful vision we've created? Some people will question whether values can affect real-world issues like success and results. Based on Luman International's experience with many organizations and thousands of leaders, our answer is a resounding, "Yes!" There is a deep and intimate connection between ethics and performance. Ethics that draw on the best in leaders, people, teams, and organizations give us a truly sustainable competitive advantage over organizations lacking a strong commitment to bedrock values.[11]

Most organizations produce lightweight statements of values that make them sound like they're loaded up with good people—but not necessarily with *effective* people. Values statements don't actually do anything to drive performance unless they're *designed* to do so. Our values should be solid, provocative, and differentiated—ideas that inspire progress instead of boring people with shallow predictability.

How Are We Going to Set Strategy, Goals, and Objectives and Establish Tactics That Will Allow Us to Arrive Successfully at Our Destination?

Once we know where we're going, what we need to do to get there, and how we're going to act and interact while we're doing it, we need to know how we're going to exercise strategies and tactics on the ground level. This is where we live out the answers to the other Big Questions.

Strategy should center on implementation, execution, and transformation. Implementation starts very early, when we involve people in answering the first four questions, and it is only successful when everyone knows their necessary contribution beforehand. Execution means we stop focusing on "roles and responsibilities" and start focusing on action and results. Transformation reminds us that the goal of strategy isn't to allow for change or survive change or even thrive during change. Passionate leaders know this: *either you're exploiting change, or it's exploiting you.*

If we can't answer these 5 questions, we have a *really* serious, festering problem.

Ask Big Questions, Get Big Answers

As a member of Sandpipers, Rosalie Puleo had realized that the group lacked a team orientation and the ability to focus on a common goal.

While the members were all wonderful and generous women, this philanthropic organization needed a specific direction and aim, Puleo concluded. "They had lost sight of why they were there," she recalls.

What dollar amount did they want to set as their projected donation for the year to the Hoag Cancer Center, and how much funding did they want to raise to meet that goal?

"We had to keep our eyes on what the purpose was," she says. Once they had the goal clearly before them—to raise money for a cancer center—they took their fund-raising to new heights, says Puleo, who also serves as a director within a very large healthcare organization. Their common purpose gave them a fresh orientation to teamwork. At every meeting, they outlined where they were with their fundraising efforts. They defined committees, rolled out responsibility, and accomplished what they set out to do.

"Once we focused on what needed to be done, we were able to do it," she says. "Over a two-year period, as president of the Sandpipers," Puleo says, "I had the privilege of leading this large group of women in raising money for the Hoag Cancer Center in Newport Beach." Finding a shared vision and a strategy to achieve it allowed them to make two very large contributions to a significant cause.

It's a story Puleo has also witnessed in business. When her employer built an online interface for healthcare providers, the plan seemed to offer more efficiency for everyone. Instead of calling in to process claims with provider representatives, providers could simply access the site.

But things didn't quite go as expected. "Healthcare is a 'high-touch' process, and online is 'low-touch,'" says Puleo. "We lost a lot of our camaraderie with our physicians at that point." The executive team set out to restore the high-touch relationships with the providers.

"Again, we had to look at the big picture," Puleo observes. "What were we doing? What

were we not doing? And how was it affecting our customers-physicians?"

The company wanted to provide enhanced service processes and help their healthcare providers care for patients. They rolled out a new "high-touch" approach in several markets, based on their return to that big answer.

"Clinicians are high-touch, and they want to have that type of environment to feel that they have a relationship with the organization," she says. Putting a service-driven vision ahead of internal programs, says Puleo, has been "very successful." The Sandpipers might say the same thing.

Rule 5: Remember That Clarity Matters

Answering the Big Questions together produces the kind of clarity that allows everyone either to affirm the chosen direction or leave the building. It's the death both of an organization's soul *and* of individual souls when people try to work toward something in which they don't believe.

THE BIG QUESTIONS

Find your organization's current vision and/or mission statement (even if you have to dig through a dusty file cabinet or two). How effectively does it answer each of the Big Questions? Be as specific as you can in your critique.

Why are we here? (Vision/Purpose)

Where are we going? (Vision/Direction)

What are we going to do to make it to this destination? (Mission)

How are we going to act and interact in order to reach our destination? (Values & Behaviors)

How are we going to set goals and objectives and establish tactics that will allow us to arrive successfully at our destination? (Strategy)

"IF I WERE TO WISH FOR ANYTHING I SHOULD NOT WISH FOR WEALTH OR POWER, BUT FOR THE PASSIONATE SENSE OF WHAT CAN BE, FOR THE EYE, WHICH, EVER YOUNG AND ARDENT, SEES THE POSSIBLE. PLEASURE DISAPPOINTS, POSSIBILITY NEVER. AND WHAT WINE IS SO INTOXICATING AS POSSIBILITY?"

SØREN KIERKEGAARD, DANISH PHILOSOPHER[12]

The Draw of a Powerful Vision

"I'll get to a place where I'm holding a conference in my head about how I want something to work," says Rodger Ferris, *"or a happy accident will take place that changes the whole direction of a piece for the better. This is what I love about making artwork."*

Ferris, a 3-D artist for Air Cabin Engineering, has done 3-D game modeling and texturing for consoles like PlayStation® 2, Xbox®, and Nintendo® Gamecube for organizations such as Walt Disney Computer Software and Sony Computer Entertainment of America.

"When I am deep into a piece I'm working on, when I'm firing on all cylinders, I can feel my consciousness being transformed," he says.

But Ferris nearly missed his calling as a professional artist.

Growing up as a child, he was good at entertaining himself in his "own world." He spent hours drawing, an interest he picked up from his grandmother, who was a painter. But once he reached high school, the idea of making a career as an artist seemed unrealistic. He recalls hearing the word "artist" attached to "starving"—and he wasn't interested in that.

So, he says, "I did what everyone does when they fear the unknown future: do what your dad does."

Ferris went to Whittier College to study business administration. "To this day, I cannot tell you what that is," he says. "Basically I learned how to party." He liked courses in philosophy, art history, and writing. Unfortunately, his business major didn't require those courses.

After his second year at Whittier, he had financial problems and withdrew. Ferris now believes that the crisis helped him rediscover that his real passion was art.

He started teaching himself to paint—abstract, colorful pieces—and the more he painted, the more he enjoyed it. He took a Saturday class at Otis Parsons, then a drawing class at Long Beach City College.

Through a friend of his father, Ferris met an artist named Don Puttman, a Western painter and instructor at Art Center College of Design. One day, they went over to Puttman's house, and he showed Ferris his work and the world in which he lived. That day, Ferris decided what he wanted to do with his life: "I was going to be an artist, no matter what," he recalls.

Ferris decided he belonged at the Art Center College of Design, a place he calls the "Shangri-la of all art schools." He was drawn to Art Center by the school's powerful vision of excellence that translated into a top-tier reputation. Talking to the counselors, he discovered that he needed to submit a portfolio for acceptance—an obstacle that most applicants never cleared.

For a year, he worked during the day and went to Art Center part-time at night, gaining the skills to put his portfolio together. At the end of the process, he was accepted to attend full time.

"This place was not for the light-hearted," says Ferris. "Only about 60 percent of the people I started with finished with me. The instructors were working artists who could really be brutal during critiques. This approach just made me stay up later than most to do better, more bullet-proof work."

The students and faculty at Art Center aligned around the school's vision, propelling the demanding culture of excellence.

"It was at Art Center that I met people I really related to," Ferris says. He graduated with honors and carried Art Center's ethos and vision into his career. "When you are passionate about something, you really excel!"

Phase 2: Starting the Revolution

THE FOUR PHASES OF FORGING A SHARED VISION:
Preparing the troops
> STARTING THE REVOLUTION
Stirring the revolution
Keeping the revolution alive

Once we've prepared the troops, we're ready to start a revolution – not, of course, a blanket revolt against authority and structure, but instead an incisive movement against the obstacles that limit us–our professional lives and our organization's passion, thinking, and performance. We're going to eliminate anything that takes away from those essential elements.

Step 1: Start at the Top?

People often ask, "Where does this revolution need to start?" Does it really need to start at the top? Most people think so. Often, however, the top isn't ready for revolution. In fact, that may be the *last* place for revolution because many there may be very happy with their positions, even if they aren't happy with the results that are being produced. They may need help to move beyond whatever they've been doing that has carried them to where they are.

So where does this revolution need to start? Where do we begin forging this shared vision? The top, the middle, or the bottom? The answer is, "Absolutely." Start at the top – *and* the middle, *and* the bottom. Wherever we can find a beachhead. Wherever we can find a foothold. Wherever we can find a few people who are willing to find a way to the future.

We don't need to enlist 40 or 50 percent of an organization to begin forging a new shared vision. We just need to start with 5 percent who are passionate, committed, true believers.

We have to find a point of entry. If it's the top, if it's the bottom, if it's a few leaders from each level–wherever it is, we have to find a point of entry to start the revolution. We can't just talk about a revolution. We actually have to start a revolution with anyone who will join. Someone has to ignite the match. Somebody has to move this organization forward. Why not you?

Step 2: Create the Case for Revolution

We have to build a case for why a revolution is necessary. "We need to do this because we have [lost market share, lost revenue, lost sales, had high turnover]." Or, "We need to do this because [our current good plan won't work when the market changes in the next two years, or we can dramatically increase our already good results, or our success is blinding us to even better opportunities]." People have to understand that the current situation – however undesirable *or* desirable – can't be changed by wishful thinking.

Creating the case for revolution requires a 3-part campaign. It's easy to cut this short, but we have to remember that cutting this campaign by 10 percent to save a month might cut our future short by decades. Here's what we need to do:

- First we make the head case, a logical and analytical explanation of the current situation and its causes and what needs to be done.

- Next is the heart case, which focuses on the passion and commitment necessary for successful change. It answers the questions, "Why should I care? How will this change affect me? How will it affect others, both inside and outside the organization?"
  Part of the heart case includes showing people that this product or service contributes to things that matter. For example, people might see building plastic lawn chairs as no big deal. But through a partnership with Free Wheelchair Mission[13] (an organization that puts wheels on chairs for people with disabilities in the developing world), people building lawn chairs feel caught up in something that lasts. It goes beyond consumerism without devaluing running a business. – Phil

- Third is the will case for change. The revolution can't stop with the head and the heart. Even if people agree with change rationally and emotionally, they might not have the will to implement it. Performance demands courage to put into practice the plans of the head and the passions of the heart. We have to attack the things that cause people to fear so we can encourage them to take at least a little personal risk to make things better.

Keep in mind, this "case for revolution" is not something we should think about just once when an organization is starting up or hitting a strategic inflection point and then we're done forever. Organizations need continual renewal, as we've seen in the automobile, airline, communications technology, retail, and other industries. As we write this book, General Motors, Dell, Intel and other former groundbreakers are struggling once again to figure out why they're here, where they're going, what they're going to do to achieve the vision, how they're going to act and interact, and what kinds of strategies and tactics work. They are trying to find new answers to the Big Questions, because the old answers no longer work.

Life changes. Markets change. Industries change. People change. Organizations change–or die. U.S. President Thomas Jefferson wrote, "Forbid we should ever be twenty years without…a rebellion."[14] That admonition applies to organizations, too, and is needed perhaps even more frequently. And each time we re-ignite a revolution, we have to build a case that draws others in. Jefferson added, "The tree of Liberty must be refreshed from time to time with the blood of patriots."[14] Fortunately, organizational liberty is refreshed by our unshakeable commitment to make things better, rather than requiring bloodshed. Real organizational "death" – terminations and layoffs – usually occurs because no one had the courage to build a timely case for needed revolution.

Step 3: Build a Band of Revolutionaries

We can't a have a revolution without revolutionaries. We need to build a Band of Revolutionaries–people who believe in the necessity of forging a new shared vision and are willing to commit themselves, their lives and their time. Revolutionaries aren't people who are ordered to start or join a revolution. They voluntarily advance in the new direction. They simply decide, "I want to be one of the people who makes this happen."

Of course, there is risk involved in such a commitment. Maybe others will feel threatened when we seek to create needed change. Maybe they'll misunderstand our motives. Maybe they'll oppose us.

American sage Henry David Thoreau observed, "Any man more right than his neighbors constitutes a majority of one already."[15] The person with a vision for what the organization can become and the courage to act has a force that everyone else, no matter how educated or experienced, does not have. One gracious, passionate, persistent person at any level can spark the revolution and draw others in with the power of truth and possibility.

A Vision for Innovation

"I view it as a challenge and passion to engage a diverse team of people to create a new marketing platform and win where no one has won before," says Christine Sakdalan, Vice President of Strategy and Client Development for Big Communications.

In her previous role—Executive Director for Marketing Innovation for Novartis Pharmaceuticals—Sakdalan had a chance to do just that. She had just finished leading a team that had responsibility for turning a brand into a blockbuster in a declining market.

After they took peak annual sales from $250 million to $1 billion within 2 years, Sakdalan was asked to build the Marketing Innovation team from the ground up. The new team had to transform the brand strategy and marketing plan, a task that pitted them against the status quo.

"People tend to be risk-averse, only doing what is proven in the marketplace," Sakdalan observes. "Because we were Marketing Innovation, we tended to offer things that were outside the box."

Sakdalan started with a few innovative hires as she put the group together. "I made sure they were from diverse backgrounds," she says. "I didn't want to get everyone from a pharmaceutical industry or we'd get the same type of thinking. I wanted, for example, expertise in relationship marketing. The best industries doing that were the financial and hotel industries. I picked someone from the hotel industry."

Sakdalan made sure her diverse team was immersed in the business realities of the pharmaceutical industry. They put together their vision and mission statement.

"Our vision statement revolved around innovation—balanced with the need to prove return on investment," she says. "It wasn't innovation for innovation's sake. It was innovation with the goal of breaking through and delivering business results. That was a unique combination."

Then they hit the ground running.

"The team came together when we had early wins," Sakdalan recalls. "I always said that we should follow the 'Giuliani principle': Do what is going to be visible right away, like getting rid of graffiti. That was Giuliani's quick win when he was Mayor of New York. When you're building a group like this, you have to be able to show those quick wins. You gain credibility and become entrenched because you're proving yourself to the larger organization."

Six months after the group formed, they already had won enough credibility to be invited into the corporate budgeting process. "You have to prove that you can deliver," she says. "Then you can do whatever you want."

Integrated with the rest of the organization, the group became the center of influence for innovation. Sakdalan recalls her excitement when her people working on multicultural marketing won a budget to do innovative insight-mining among Spanish speakers. She traces her group's success to the vision that brought them together.

"It is truly exciting and gratifying to see a new organization come to life with a mission and a vision," she says. "Always keep that end goal in mind. Stay passionate about that goal. Sometimes, as you're going through a difficult challenge or through a process, it's hard to keep your eye on the prize. Keep that perspective, and you can weed out the unimportant."

Step 4: Educate Deeply and Widely at All Levels

Once it's formed, the Band of Revolutionaries has to educate the organization deeply and widely–anyone who'll listen, even if they're skeptical. They're going to have to talk about this revolution and address people's legitimate concerns, doubts, and emotional reactions.

Because of the uniqueness of every individual and organization, this process has to be organic rather than structured and mechanical. A formula can't replace person-to-person interaction, especially when one party is a passionate revolutionary and the other is a doubter. Each revolutionary has to take on as a personal mission the task of showing several people the need for a fresh direction, a new shared vision.

Step 5: Design an Internal Benchmark

Many people will refuse to change until they understand how serious the need for change is. That reality means that (as much as possible) we have to define the present state of the organization as part of our case for change. We have to design an internal benchmark. We have to know where we are, so we can see how far we really have to go. This analysis of the starting condition of the organization will allow us to gauge what needs to change and whether those changes are actually making things better or worse as we go along.

> **"MEN WHO BLAZED NEW PATHS FOR CIVILIZATION HAVE ALWAYS BEEN PRECEDENT BREAKERS. IT IS EVER THE MAN WHO BELIEVES IN HIS OWN IDEAS; WHO CAN THINK AND ACT WITHOUT A CROWD TO BACK HIM; WHO IS NOT AFRAID TO STAND ALONE; WHO IS BOLD, ORIGINAL, RESOURCEFUL; WHO HAS THE COURAGE TO GO WHERE OTHERS HAVE NEVER BEEN, TO DO THINGS THAT LEAVE HIS MARK ON HIS TIMES.**
> **DON'T WAIT FOR EXTRAORDINARY OPPORTUNITIES.**
> **SEIZE COMMON ONES AND MAKE THEM UNCOMMON."**
> **ORISON SWETT MARDEN, AUTHOR**[16]

Phase 3: Stirring the Revolution

THE FOUR PHASES OF FORGING A SHARED VISION:
Preparing the troops
Starting the revolution
> **STIRRING THE REVOLUTION**
Keeping the revolution alive

Step 1: Secure Senior Leadership Neutrality

Senior leadership at first might be cautious and skeptical or even hostile to major change. Whether it includes senior leaders or not, the Band of Revolutionaries has to take the time to secure senior leadership neutrality—at the very least. It's very difficult to forge a shared vision if the senior leadership actively opposes the initiative or promotes an alternative "holding action."

Take the Ford Mustang as an example. Don Frey, project manager for this highly successful new car in the early 1960s, recalled, "The whole project was bootlegged. There was no official approval of this thing. We had to do it on a shoestring." He kept the project a secret, with his team working nights and weekends off-site so he could avoid what he called "administrivia." Ford management was still burned by the failure of the Edsel, an earlier venture into the "new," and Frey didn't want to risk their crushing the vision–a vision responsible for two thirds of Ford's profits in the Mustang's first year on the market.[17]

And so the senior leadership at least needs to be convinced to stand aside. Neutralizing opposition might mean presenting the case for revolution to the senior leadership. It might include showing them an early picture of what the organization could become and the kind of results that it could achieve. A test case can be very effective if one exists.

And if you are in senior leadership and have doubts, that's okay–just try to hold your fire until the revolution is strong enough to show what it can do.

Step 2: Partner with the Human Investment Team

An essential component of a revolution needs to be a shift in how we think about people. We need to think about people as investors (thinking, choice-enabled human beings) rather than as resources (inanimate, consumable objects).

The "people" people (better called the "Human Investment Team" instead of "Human Resources") need to be strategically involved in forging the shared vision. Partner with them and help them understand that their role is not just to police the organization but to help you forge a people-friendly image of the future that senior leadership can get behind.

Step 3: Involve for Be-In™, Don't Sell for "Buy-In"

Work hard for full involvement. And remember that informing is *not* involving. Telling people what we're going to do isn't really involving them. Instead, they need to have a real say, a real opportunity to make this revolution better and make it their own.

In his autobiography, actor Alan Alda observes, "Real listening is a willingness to let the other person change you."[18] Dialogue is more than informational exchanges and issuing communiqués. People's input to the process will make them more passionate and will make the process itself more refined and effective. Actually involving people creates *Be-In*™—real investment, real commitment—while selling a canned vision aims only for getting buy-in—lip service, no open disagreement. When people know that they are free to add value to the process, that there's a safe way for them to step forward, they will join in and help us win.

Step 4: Develop the Formal Revolutionary Charter

It's time to produce an actual document, a revolutionary charter. At Luman International, we've worked with many organizations to create a Vision, Mission, Values, and Behaviors (*VMVB*™) charter and the supporting mechanisms to make it effective. This charter announces with a united voice, "This may not be where we are today, but this is who we're going to be."

The settlers sailing to the New World from Europe knew that they needed to have a statement of why and how they would live together. In the same way, we have to recognize the value of having a written document that commits us to a common future. The Pilgrims on the *Mayflower* produced the Mayflower Compact, a social contract that would be a decisive factor for success in the untamed country that had beaten those who'd come before them. They were right. A revolutionary charter can be the same kind of guide for us, holding our organization together as we face the unforeseen dangers of a strange new land.

When we explore new territory in pursuit of a fresh vision, we may be operating in areas about which little good information exists. When Ferdinand Magellan set off to sail around the world, the maps of the New World—especially the South American coast he would have to navigate—were little more than guesses built on a few bits of information from pilots who had been there before. But Magellan and his crew put together new maps that could be improved upon by future explorers. They created a viable starting point for future exploration. Living the revolutionary charter might mean making new maps—producing information about what works that those who follow us can refine.

Step 5: Spread the Revolution

When we've taken these steps, we might find ourselves with a full-blown revolution. So what's next? It's time to *expand* it. We have to keep talking about it and bringing it up at meetings when decisions are made. We can ask questions like, "How does this possibility align with our charter?" and "Is this decision really going to help us reach our destination?" The *VMVB*™ charter has to become part of the organization's daily life to avoid the tragedy of becoming just a plaque on the wall.

Chartering a Triumph

In March 2003, Dave Hager was named Senior Vice President in charge of exploration and production activities for Kerr-McGee Corporation, a large independent oil and gas exploration and production company.

"I felt well-qualified and was excited to lead this organization," he says.

But almost immediately, Hager faced some tough challenges.

The organization had strong technical professionals in every relevant discipline and had developed some very creative technical advances that were admired throughout the industry. It also had hard working, committed, highly ethical employees. Hager had worked for years with many of the people he was now leading, and he was confident that he had their respect and support.

However, the stock price had been lagging behind the organization's peers in the industry for a long time. People felt frustrated that internal change had not yet made a difference, and many believed that top-tier performance would require a new strategy.

Solving these dilemmas became Hager's passion. He wanted each person to look back on a career with Kerr-McGee and know the effort was worth it—and to have operational and financial successes to prove it.

"These people had been my friends for many years, and I wanted to help them succeed in every way," he explains.

With input from everyone in the organization, they developed a new vision and mission, as well as a set of values and behaviors that were important for achieving the desired results. "We had many open, frank discussions, and were able to get down to the unvarnished truth regarding our strengths and weaknesses," he recalls. Each employee had at least three "touches"—opportunities to comment and suggest changes—and took ownership of the process.

They memorialized the results in a small pamphlet that employees carried with them or kept in their offices. It outlined the key values that they had mutually agreed were important to their organization—value creation, integrity and trust, respect, communication, excellence, passion, and teamwork—and what they would do to demonstrate these values.

Then they started putting the new vision, mission, strategy, and set of beliefs to work. Hager remembers that it wasn't easy. The organization sold off assets that did not fit their new strategy and purchased others. They changed the way they worked with each other and challenged each other to do better. They eliminated unnecessary processes and developed new ones that were critical to their results. The few employees who did not fit into this new approach left.

Kerr-McGee emerged a stronger, more nimble company, and the results spoke for themselves. Their respect in the investment community increased dramatically. The employees were justifiably proud of the results and the role they had played.

And during this 3-year period, the stock price increased over 300 percent, leading the peer group, and the company became a first-quartile performer.

As a result of this dramatic turnaround, Hager was promoted to Chief Operating Officer. In June, 2006, the company received an all-cash offer for a 40 percent premium over the current stock price.

What stands out for Hager is the pride his people gained through the process of chartering a new vision and acting on it.

"They deserved all they received," says Hager, "and I was grateful for the small role I had in helping them achieve these results."

DRAFT A CHARTER

Taking your answers to The Big Questions (page 53), write out a first draft of a new charter that addresses any gaps or inadequacies. Don't be afraid to dream big.

Vision/Purpose

Vision/Direction

Mission

Values & Behaviors

Strategy

"LET YOUR IMAGINATION DRIVE YOUR VISION."
SUSAN CLAMPITT

Phase 4: Keeping the Revolution Alive

THE FOUR PHASES OF FORGING A SHARED VISION:
Preparing the troops
Starting the revolution
Stirring the revolution
> KEEPING THE REVOLUTION ALIVE

Step 1: Commission a Sustaining Team

A Sustaining Team should carry on the revolutionary tradition of the Band of Revolutionaries within the newly chartered organization. The Team should focus on asking the hard questions: Are we living this $VMVB^{™}$? Are we practicing it in our team and in our individual decision making? Is it really part of the life of our organization? Let the Sustaining Team create their own supporting charter and rotate members so that fresh ideas and excitement continually feed into the momentum created by the original Band. It is this team's duty to pump innovation constantly into the ongoing revolution.

Step 2: Re-commission the Human Investment Team

Re-commission the Human Investment Team (formerly known as "Human Resources") to make the shared $VMVB^{™}$ part of their performance-agreement process, their performance-leadership system, their thinking about who gets hired and who gets promoted. Is this shared vision guiding our daily actions and decisions about people? Is it guiding *their* actions and decisions? The HI Team can codify what the revolution produced.

Step 3: Measure and Modify

Revisit the internal benchmark and measure whether anything is changing. Take an organization-wide survey focused on the $VMVB^{™}$ at six months, a year, and every year after that. We have to find out how we're living the vision—badly, well, or in-between. Down the road, if the organization is still falling short or even dropping off in how it's living this shared vision, we can take action to modify our actions or any deficiencies in the *VMVB*™. Make it come alive and invite passionate people to help you renew the process.

Step 4: Watch the Connection between Your VMVB™ and Intelligent Growth™

Don't forget: A powerful *VMVB*™ allows great organizations to grow intelligently far into the future. Not all growth is positive--cancer grows rapidly and without restriction. *Intelligent Growth*™, on the other hand, is guided and controlled by the *VMVB*™.

This *VMVB*™-*centered Intelligent Growth*™ is fully integrated with your cultural drivers, and it's renewable and sustainable through your focus on *Truth Capital*™, *Passion Capital*™, *Thinking Capital*™, and *Performance Capital*™. (Measuring these forms of capital is critical--even though most organizations don't.)[19]

Keeping a Powerful Vision Fresh

Rob Nicolosi's grandfather, Isadore Salvatore Nicolosi, founded Nicolosi Foods in 1952 on Webster Avenue in the Bronx. Now operating in Union City, New Jersey, the company has thrived in a niche market of a tough industry by restructuring around a fresh, compelling vision that maintains longstanding values.

His grandfather's "honesty and care for his customers, in addition to his knowledge of the industry, gave him great success," recalls Nicolosi, the third-generation owner, President and CEO of the company. These values still guide the company, he says. But Nicolosi has faced the challenge of finding new ways to practice these values in a changing industry, one in which the competition has consolidated and big companies dominate.

"I saw that if we didn't start changing, we wouldn't be around for many years to come," he notes. "We wanted to be old in nature and tradition but new in mission. I learned about hard work from my family, to do things cost-effectively, and to not avoid getting your hands dirty. I still get involved in the day-to-day activities. But those are only going to take you so far. Complacency is a bad place to be."

For Nicolosi, avoiding complacency has meant introducing high-quality products that offer premium flavor and healthy, all-natural ingredients—products that larger producers often cannot afford to imitate.

"What our children are eating needs to be healthy. We're trying to educate the consumers about what they're putting into their own and their children's mouths," he says. But even the new products get tied to the company's past and its values.

"We're carrying the tradition of family values on our labels," says Nicolosi. "There's a nutrient mark on it, as well as a picture of my two eldest daughters." The motto: "Work to live, not live to work."

There's another tradition Nicolosi carries forward: the mentoring he received from his grandfather, father, and uncle, who taught him to work hard, plan ahead, face problems head on, and live with good character. He now has the opportunity to mentor many of his employees, several of whom are first-generation immigrants like his grandfather. The company offers them extra support and training, and Nicolosi himself gets to know them as he works with them.

"You have to create a family environment, caring about your workers and relating to them. We're all here to do the same job, so you have to stand side-by-side with them to cut meat or pack the product," he says. "They realize that you're not afraid to work. It's a team effort, and you have to communicate that."

It's this focus on old values, along with evolving knowledge and business-model advancements, that carries Nicolosi Foods into the twenty-first century. Over half a century old, the company is still young with a powerful vision.

"We're here to make a profit but also to grow a legacy, to build a brand and something that you believe in," says Nicolosi. "I hope to pass it on to my kids."

INVESTING IN YOUR ORGANIZATION'S VISION

What about *you*, one individual in the entire organization? What part can just one person play? There are 4 stages in the process of forging a shared vision in your organization. And you have an important role in each.

LET'S LOOK AT EACH ONE IN MORE DETAIL SO YOU CAN SEE HOW TO DO IT.

Stage 1: Agitating for Change

> **THE FOUR STAGES OF INVESTING IN THE VISION:**
> **> AGITATING FOR CHANGE**
>   Evaluating the cost
>   Participating in the process
>   Living the vision

In the first stage, your organization doesn't have a shared vision and doesn't seem likely to forge one any time soon. What role can you play? You're just one person. But here's the news: *every* revolution starts with just one person.

We've heard hundreds of people say, "What can I do? I'm not the CEO or COO or Executive Director. I don't have a position of final authority." But there is seldom anyone with "final authority." Even CEOs have people to whom they're responsible. Everyone has boundaries. Everyone has restrictions. Everyone has reasons and potential excuses not to participate.

When Florence Nightingale, the English visionary who founded modern nursing, was asked near the end of her life if she could condense the reason for her success down to one principle, her response was crisp: "I never gave or took any excuse."[20] No excuses. We've only got one crack at this business called "life," and we don't want to waste it making excuses that lead to mediocrity and regret.

Mahatma Gandhi had no formal position of power when he revolutionized India. Martin Luther King, Jr., had no formal position of power when he revolutionized race relations in the United States, nor did Nelson Mandela as he helped bring down apartheid in South Africa. Mandela had been a prisoner for 27 years!

Vaclav Havel, the Czech poet, had no position of authority (he was a poet!). Yet he joined the revolution against the Communist regime in Czechoslovakia and became the first president of the Czechoslovak Federative Republic. Lech Walesa was a Polish electrician from the Gdansk shipyard (not much of a position of authority!) and yet he led the revolution against communism in Poland, a revolution that eventually spread throughout Eastern Europe and toppled the Berlin Wall. An actor, Ronald Reagan stood almost alone in his conviction that the stranglehold of Soviet tyranny could be broken—and then led the effort to break it. No one ever is "too small."

So when we say we don't have any power to cause change, we're missing the power of one person. Playwright George Bernard Shaw said, "People are always blaming their circumstances for what they are. I do not believe in circumstances. The people who get on in this world are the people who get up and look for the circumstances they want, and if they cannot find them, make them."

If your organization doesn't have a shared vision, or if the vision it has is no longer meaningful or applicable in the real world, then you can be the person to start the revolution. At Luman International, we've seen these revolutions begin with one informal leader in the middle of an organization who finally decides, "This is not an acceptable way for me to live. This is not an acceptable way for our organization to live."[22]

You can be the one. You can agitate for change and persuade people that there is a better way to live. You can be an effective agitator. There are 7 keys to *effective* agitation:

> "DEEP CHANGE REQUIRES MORE THAN THE IDENTIFICATION OF THE PROBLEM AND A CALL FOR ACTION. IT REQUIRES LOOKING BEYOND THE SCOPE OF THE PROBLEM AND FINDING THE ACTUAL SOURCE OF THE TROUBLE. THE REAL PROBLEM IS FREQUENTLY LOCATED WHERE WE WOULD LEAST EXPECT TO FIND IT, INSIDE OURSELVES . . . . IT MEANS SOMEONE MUST BE ENORMOUSLY SECURE AND COURAGEOUS. CULTURE CHANGE STARTS WITH PERSONAL CHANGE. . . . ULTIMATELY, THE PROCESS RETURNS US TO THE 'POWER OF ONE.'" ROBERT E. QUINN[21]

Effective Agitation Key 1: Be Gracious

You have to carry on this kind of a revolution with grace. A revolutionary is trying to deal the existing mediocre organization a life-changing blow, but the iron fist has to wear a velvet glove. You want to step on people's shoes without messing up their shine. You're going to get enough reactions from people clinging to the status quo without making your own contribution to the problem.

You have to be gracious.
Other people need to know you're not out for yourself. Effective agitation can't be a self-centered, ambitious, promote-my-own-agenda campaign that tears other people down on its path to victory. It has to be designed for everyone's good.

At Luman International, there's a point we always make with our consulting clients: "We're here for everyone's good. We're a consulting practice that will not give individual recommendations on people – should you keep them, should you get rid of them. We're here not to hurt *anyone* but to help ***everyone***. We're here to assist the whole cause." People in these organizations know that it's safe to work with us because we're here with no agenda other than the success of the entire team. That's the approach that works with transformation and revolution.

The only people you won't appear to be helping are the 5 percent who are bad apples; you're taking away their forum for complaint. Ultimately, however, you even help them because they'll either make the internal change necessary to join the revolution or leave and find a place that suits them.

As you present your 3-part case for change (see above, page 56 & 57), you have to package your revolutionary ideas in such a way that people can hear them. You can't be disrespectful to authority. You may have great ideas, but if you deliver them with anger, rage, and cynicism, no one can hear you. Human beings are sensitive. Maybe they've invested a lot in the way things currently are, and you're throwing a spear through that comfort zone. To win their hearts and minds, you can't attack the status quo in a way that appears to be tearing down their position, their authority, their dignity, or their identity.

Effective Agitation Key 2: Establish Your Own Mindset
Establish your own firm mindset. Too many people throw their hands up and say, "It is what it is." This is a healthy statement of fact if we're talking about facing reality but a terrible argument against trying to improve. Determine for yourself that what "is" is unacceptable and that what "should be" ***can*** be achieved. Decide that you will be the one, and that you will not be dissuaded. Set your mind to persist until something changes.

Don't be satisfied until you take the mountain and move it. Don't settle for moving molehills. Promise yourself, "I'm going to keep my eye on the big picture. I'm not going be distracted, not by a promotion, not by a reassignment, not by people who warn me. I firmly believe that what 'is' is unacceptable and that what 'should be' ***can*** be, ***will*** be, and ***must*** be."

Effective Agitation Key 3: Educate Yourself about Shared Vision and Values

Educate yourself about the power of shared vision. Look at other revolutionary *VMVB*™ statements. Find out which organizations have visions and values that really are driving forces and what people did to create those visions and determine those values. Your own passion and commitment will be insufficient to move the mountain if your ideas are not fully informed. Go to work, and find out what works and what doesn't work.

Effective Agitation Key 4: Find Like-minded Revolutionaries

Effective agitation includes finding potential fellow revolutionaries. Put out the word and see who wants to join the Underground—not to spread questionable information through the *grapevine* but to bring purpose and vision back into organizational life through the organizational **lifeline**.

Don't just test for whether they share your ideas but for whether they share your *passion*. People can give mental and verbal assent ("Yes, that sounds like a good idea") when they have no intention of doing anything except jumping on the bandwagon after it's fully moving. At this point, you need people who are willing to push-start the wagon, not just get a free ride after the toil and sweat have been spent by others.

Effective Agitation Key 5: Create a Mini-Charter

Create your own miniature *VMVB*™. In your case for revolution, your little Band will need its own mini-charter. What are you going to do to agitate for change? All great revolutionaries have had manifestos. They've all known what they wanted to accomplish. You'll have to answer the same questions. It will remind you of what you're trying to accomplish. It will keep the powers-that-be from sidetracking you.

It will also give you practice drafting charters, so when the leadership finally agrees with you and says, "We need this. How do we do it?" you will already have created and lived your own mini-*VMVB*™ with your fellow revolutionaries

Effective Agitation Key 6: Practice Creative Tenacity

You and your associate revolutionaries will need *creative tenacity*™. If you approach a certain senior leader and continue to get resistance, either find a different way to approach that leader or approach different leaders. Just being tenacious without being creative is craziness. It's doing the same thing over and over again and hoping to get a different result – but all you really get is a headache.

With creative tenacity, it's amazing how quickly we can get to a tipping point. At Luman International, we have seen bottom-quartile organizations with anywhere from 1,500 to 10,000 people turned around by 15 or 20 people who had enough creative tenacity to start moving the entire ship in a different direction.

Effective Agitation Key 7: Expect Rejection

You are taking risks here, so you will have to expect rejection. Revolutionary leaders understand that they may lose many battles on the way to winning the war. As George Newman writes, "Successful people receive the most rejections. . . . They have figured out that it doesn't matter how often you hear *no* – what's important is to keep asking until you hear *yes*."[23]

You know that your agitation is winning when you hear a senior leader who has not been engaged in the process asking you or another senior leader, "What is all this revolution stuff that I keep hearing about?"

> "IF ONE ADVANCES CONFIDENTLY IN THE DIRECTION OF HIS DREAMS, AND ENDEAVORS TO LIVE THE LIFE WHICH HE HAS IMAGINED, HE WILL MEET WITH A SUCCESS UNEXPECTED IN COMMON HOURS."
>
> **HENRY DAVID THOREAU**[24]

Stage 2: Evaluating the Cost

THE FOUR STAGES OF INVESTING IN THE VISION:
Agitating for change
> **EVALUATING THE COST**
Participating in the process
Living the vision

So what do you do if the organization refuses to forge a new, shared vision? What do you do if they reject your proposal? While you're practicing creative tenacity, remember that some wars take a long time and you may have just signed up for a long tour of duty.

Few things of value are won easily. Many things fail because no one persists past the first rejection. A few things succeed because someone just won't quit.

Step 1: Make a Commitment for the Long Haul

The first thing you have to do is make a commitment: "I'm in this for the long haul. I've been rejected, but things change. Circumstances change. Attitudes change. Leaders change."

Keep the hope of a vision alive. Keep talking about it. You might need to change the way you agitate, perhaps not pursuing the goal as overtly. But find ways to drop examples into conversations and make suggestions in acceptable settings. Time and circumstances may be on your side.

Step 2: Change Your Piece of the World

Create a "pilot plant" in your own part of the organization. Whether there are two of you or a thousand of you in your unit, department, or division, forge a shared vision in your area. This means that one thing is certain, and another is possible:

1. You're going to achieve better results because you will all be on the same page.
2. As your results improve and you begin to out-perform other departments or divisions, since success speaks so loudly, people in other parts of the organization or even the senior leadership might say, "I don't know what you're doing, but we better do it everywhere." It can reopen the doors.

Step 3: Be Shrewd

Don't brag about the successes in your area too much. Don't allow an opening for others to think of you as proud and arrogant. Let the results speak for themselves.

Step 4: Be Willing To Move On

What happens if the organization won't allow you to forge a shared vision even in your own area? At some point you have to say, "This is no longer a viable country. I have to find the Statue of Liberty. I have to go where there is freedom, where there is opportunity to do what's important."

At the point where you can neither talk about vision nor implement it, you need to evaluate what the organization is doing to your personal life and passion. In the right organization, your voice will matter and your passion will be valued. (For more on finding an organization that aligns with your passion, see **The Confidence Principle: Finding Your Life's Passion and a Place to Live It**, the sixth title in the PASSIONATE LIVES & LEADERS SERIES).

This will benefit your current organization as well. There's no reason to think badly about the organization or its leadership. There may be a lot of fine people in positions of authority, but they just don't see the need for what you're talking about, and because of that, they aren't going to permit great change. Everything you're talking about will become a nuisance and a frustration.

Try to find that line between creative tenacity and unfruitful stubbornness. The line is further out there than it might seem to be at first glance, but if it's there and you can see it, don't cross it. There's a better place for you.

Stage 3: Participating in the Process

THE FOUR STAGES OF INVESTING IN THE VISION:
Agitating for change
Evaluating the cost
> **PARTICIPATING IN THE PROCESS**
Living the vision

They've said, "Let's do it." The organization or your part of the organization is going to forge a shared vision. What can you do to participate? What can you do to help?

A *lot*:

Step 1: Realize It Is the Chance of a Lifetime

First of all, realize that this is a rare opportunity in a career. Very few people get a chance to determine the future shape and structure of an entire organization. Grab hold of this opportunity with everything that's in you.

Step 2: Commit Big Amounts of Time

This won't last very long. It may only be a few weeks or months until this vision is put into place, so commit big amounts of time. In this season of your life, cut out the extra events, cut out extra personal time, cut out the vacations. Let your family or friends know they're not going to be seeing as much of you as usual. Don't let this opportunity get away by being unwilling to commit the time. Your passion will more than keep you going, even on long days and short sleep.

Step 3: Commit to Winning One Person at a Time

Commit to winning a person over to this process every day or every week. Go to them. Talk with them. Show them the advantages. Share what you've learned from your education, what you've seen happen in other companies, what you've learned from your reading. Revolutions are not started by winning 500 people at a time but by winning one person at a time—a person who can then start winning one *other* person at a time.

Step 4: Attend All Sessions

Attend all meetings and discussions where you can learn what other people are thinking and where you can contribute your own perspective. While those sessions are going on, graciously push for more–more dialogue, more involvement, more change. The more involvement, the more people have the opportunity to touch this process and influence this document. The *VMVB*™ will be more powerful when it's implemented because everyone will own it.

"I DON'T REALLY THINK MOST ORGANIZATIONS ARE GLUED TOGETHER WITH A VISION....AND I THINK OUR VISION HAS GROUNDED US....THE RETURN ON THAT INVESTMENT, EVEN THOUGH AT THE TIME IT LOOKED EXPENSIVE - OVER TIME IT HAS BEEN A TREMENDOUS BARGAIN. THE RETURN ON THOSE INVESTMENTS HAS JUST BEEN ENORMOUS."

JAMES B. DESTEFANO, PRESIDENT & CEO, OCCUPATIONS, INC.

Stage Four: Living the Vision

THE FOUR STAGES OF INVESTING IN THE VISION:
Agitating for change
Evaluating the cost
Participating in the process
> **LIVING THE VISION**

Once this vision has come to life, what do you do to support it?

Step 1: Bring It Up Constantly

Even if it's a plaque on the wall in the conference room, no one will look at it or read it unless somebody points it out and says, "What about this?" Every action in the organization needs to be made in the light of the new shared vision. If not, the vision will not come fully to life and it will not have full effect. Eventually, it might have **no** effect.

The organization needs to make the vision part of every decision until it becomes like breathing–normal, routine, but absolutely crucial. Every time a decision is made–for example, when choosing the advertisements for use in hiring new people or the deliverables of projects undertaken by teams–people need to ask:

- Is this action in line with our shared *VMVB*™?
- Is it part of the new 'who we are'? Or do we need to change parts of this plan?
- Does it reflect our stated values?
- Are parts of this plan moving us back to the old way because it's familiar and comfortable?

You'll have to be the one to ask the questions. You can't count on anyone else to do it. You have to help others filter everything through the vision.

Step 2: Challenge Others to Live It

Challenge others to live this vision. Challenge them to convert their negative passion about the current situation into positive passion about what the organization can be if the 95 percent would truly commit. Be willing to be the point of challenge for your entire organization.

Here are some questions to challenge those around you: "If we would really live this, what would change about our daily actions?" How much better would it be to come into work? How much more effective and powerful could we be as individuals and collectively as a team?"

Step 3: Harbor No Illusions

Lastly, encourage people to give up all illusions. Encourage them to measure how successfully the organization is living the revolutionary ***VMVB*™** charter, and when they look at the results, not to blame others or make excuses.

Show them how to acknowledge the results and say, "If there's a part of our vision, mission, values and behaviors that we're not living, there's a reason we're not living it. If we can find what that reason is, we can change it and we can begin to live the vision right now." No illusions. Only knowing the truth is going to set us free.

TIME FOR ACTION

So what have we said?

You've seen disgruntled workers. It's time now to build a place for the "gruntled"—also known as passionate people.

Once we identify and eliminate the obstacles to building a passionate organization, we have the chance to design and build one. We can create an organization in which exuberant spirits can work together to create outstanding performance where nothing existed before. If we do this, we will leave the legacy of a passionate organization.

We can design our passionate organization from the inside out, starting with culture and then moving through strategy, structure, process, people, results, and rewards.

We can build our passionate organization around 10 Key Elements that we richly incorporate into our organizational DNA.

And we can focus it all on achieving a worthy vision. Without forging a shared vision, we don't have a shot at anything but mediocrity. If someone wants a mediocre organization and mediocre results, they shouldn't forge a shared vision.

But if you want an organization that displays passionate performance, forging a shared vision will lead to better results, greater effectiveness, and a more soul-satisfying experience for the entire organization and for every individual who resides in it.

This isn't easy, which is why more leaders and organizations haven't done it. But it isn't too difficult either. You now know what can be accomplished and how to go about it. You know what it takes to design and build a passionate organization. You have a way to capture the limitless power of passion.

> **"NOTHING EXISTS WHICH EXUBERANT SPIRITS HAVE NOT HELPED TO CREATE."**
> **FRIEDRICH NIETZSCHE**

You're only one person. But you can do it.

For more on building passionate teams, see ***The Attraction Principle: Finding, Keeping, and Teaming Passionate People,*** the second title in the PASSIONATE LIVES & LEADERS SERIES.

FAQ

Isn't passion really about enthusiasm and emotion?

No. It can include these and often does, but some of the most passionate people we've known are intensely quiet and focused. It is too easy to mistake enthusiasm for passion. Enthusiasm can seem very dramatic but can fade away like an ice cube on a hot sidewalk. Passion is committed, in it for the long haul, and continues to drive even if hit with tough challenges or hard blows.

How do I know if my attempts at designing a passionate organization are working?

First, you can see it in the attitude of people about the organization, their work, and each other. Second, you should be able to see it in changes to the way people act – less infighting, less political nonsense, less gossip and grapevine, more collaboration, more mutual support, more focus on goals. And third, you can see it in quantitative measurements. Organizations test the level of "employee satisfaction" all the time. Why not the level of *Passion DNA*™ and *Passion Capital*™?

We have a current vision statement that no one really knows or cares about, but it's there. What should we do?

Most organizations have some form of vision statement or mission statement or purpose statement or philosophy statement. But it's not having the statement that makes the difference – it's having an *effective* statement that has *Be-In*™. Something written 50 years ago by the boss over martinis or 10 years ago by the senior leadership team on a retreat or 5 years ago by a consultant is almost never going to get the job done. Keep the current document in play–there's no reason to pitch out anything that's good, and it can help the acceptance of the new document to include some past references–but don't let poor or inadequate ancient history control your future.

Everybody around here talks about "values," but no one has the same list, calls them the same thing, or practices them the same way. Where should we go from here?

There's something inside of most human beings that wants to have and live a set of values or principles. But here's the deal: If we have differing values or varying definitions or random applications, then the simple fact is that *as an organization* we have no values. Having the whole organization hammer out a tight set of values with clear, concrete definitions and agreement about the behaviors that will flow from those values is a powerful exercise that no one will forget. It's a whole lot easier to talk about values than to live and die by a commonly held set of them.

I know we need to change, but do we really need all of this talk about "revolution"?

No. We can try to change modestly, and we can perhaps achieve some modest improvements as a result of our efforts. Evolutionary change can make a difference – if you have the time to wait for it. But let's face it: change is hard. Even modest change can be hard in many organizations. And the greater the number of obstacles and the bigger they are, the less likely that modest, evolutionary change will get the job done. The goal isn't to change just to be changing. The goal is to change to be *effective*. If modest change will move you up one level and that's all you want or need, then by all means take it on. But if revolutionary change can move you up 2 or 3 or 5 or 10 levels, why wouldn't you want it? Often, it's the tradeoff between the pain of change now or the pain of mediocrity or annihilation later.

We seem to be overrun by what you call "myths and illusions." What can we do?

The only safe place to start is to expose them and how strong their hold is on the organization. By their very nature, they are embedded in the team's mindset and the way it thinks about and approaches the world. And by their tenacity they can make Bruce Willis in *Die Hard* look like a Sunday-school teacher. Find a way to get some quantitative data and then build your case for change from that. Luman can help with its groundbreaking *Reality Quotient*™, an online assessment that leaves no myth or illusion safe.

For more on this powerful subject of passion, please see James Lucas's full-length book **The Passionate Organization:** *Igniting the Fire of Employee Commitment.*

Luman International also has an in-depth assessment, the Passion Quotient™, which will provide you tremendous insight into your organization's Passion DNA, Infrastructure, Leadership, People, and Transformation/Adaptive Capacity.

LUMAN®
international

We offer a full-day course, "Building a Passionate Organization," and a number of keynotes or short presentations on the topic, including "Capturing the Power of Passion™."

We can assist you on several aspects of designing and building a passionate organization with our Signature Processes, including "VMVB™ Chartering" and "Generating High Return on Human Investment (ROHI)™."

"PASSION IS THE LIFEBLOOD OF ORGANIZATIONS [AND] WHAT DIFFERENTIATES GREAT COMPANIES FROM MEDIOCRE ONES. IN AN ENLIGHTENING WAY, JAMES LUCAS DEMONSTRATES THE COMPETITIVE ADVANTAGES."

MANFRED KETS DE VRIES, CLINICAL PROFESSOR OF MANAGEMENT AND LEADERSHIP, INSEAD, FRANCE, AUTHOR OF *LEADERS, FOOLS, AND IMPOSTERS* AND *THE LEADERSHIP MYSTIQUE*

Endnotes

1. Brooker, Katrina. "Can Anyone Replace Herb?" Fortune *17 April 2000: 190.*
2. Kennedy, Randy. "My True Story, More or Less, or Maybe Not at All." New York Times. *15 Jan. 2006.*
3. Waugh, Chris. Updrafts. *Otter Rock, OR: Alberteen, 2007.*
4. Lucas, James R. Fatal Illusions: Shredding a Dozen Unrealities that Can Keep Your Organization from Success. *Kansas City: Quintessential Books, 2001.*
5. Gardner, John W. "How to Prevent Organizational Dry Rot." Harper's Magazine *Oct. 1965: 24.*
6. Wenburg, Cy. Gadflies. *Victoria, BC: Trafford, 2006.*
7. Galvani, William. Mainsail to the Wind. *Dobbs Ferry: Sheridan House, 1999.*
8. Yang, Jae and Alejandro Gonzalez, "Most Employers Don't Share Company Strategy." USA Today. *21 Nov. 2006, 1. [Source: Cognos/Palladium Group "Making Strategy Execution a Competitive Advantage" (study of 143 strategy management professionals)].*
9. Yang, Jae and Marcy E. Mullins, "What Employees Want." USA Today. *[Source: Jack Morton Experiential Marketing Global Consumer Response (survey of 1,652 workers and job seekers conducted by Sponsorship Research International)].*
10. "Starbucks CEO Applauds Staff Passion." News Tribune. *15 June 1998.*
11. Cantrell, Wes, and James R. Lucas. High-Performance Ethics: Ten Timeless Principles for Next-Generation Leadership. *Carol Stream: Tyndale, 2007.*
12. Kierkegaard, Søren. Either/Or: A Fragment of Life. *New York: Penguin Group, 1992.*
13. For more information, see www.freewheelchairmission.org/mission.html.
14. Jefferson, Thomas. Letter to William Smith. *13 Nov. 1787, manuscript. 6 Feb. 2001.* Establishing a Federal Republic. *Lib. of Congress.*
15. Thoreau, Henry David. "Civil Disobedience." *Carlisle: Applewood, 2000.*
16. Marden, Orison Swett. Pushing to the Front. *Whitefish: Kessinger, 2003.*
17. Healey, James R. "Ford's famous filly turns 40." USA Today. *16 April 2004: B-1.*
18. Alda, Alan. Never Have Your Dog Stuffed. *New York: Random House, 2005.*
19. Luman International has the only assessments of their kind to measure these four critical "non-financial" forms of capital.
20. Nightingale, Florence. Notes on Nursing. *Hicksville, NY: Dickson-Keanaghan, 2005.*
21. Quinn, Robert E. Deep Change: Discovering the Leader Within. *Hoboken: Wiley, 1996.*
22. For a chance to read these case studies, visit the Luman International website at www.lumaninternational.com.
23. Newman, George. "Sometimes It Pays to Overpay." Bottom Line. *1 Sept. 2006.*
24. Thoreau, Henry David. Walden. *New York: Houghton Mifflin, 2005.*

JAMES R. LUCAS

James R. Lucas is a recognized authority on leadership and cultural design. He is a groundbreaking author and thought leader, provocative speaker, and experienced consultant on these crucial topics.

Jim is President and CEO of Luman International, an organization which he founded in 1983. This firm is dedicated to Developing Passionate, Thinking, Pure-Performance Organizations™ and their leaders, people, and teams.

Clients are from sectors as diverse as health care, pharmaceuticals, medical devices, financial services, accounting, energy, chemicals, forest and paper products, transportation, computer hardware, diversified manufacturing, consumer products, diversified business services, construction, state government, and federal government. They range from Fortune 1000 public companies and private for-profit organizations to not-for-profits and government agencies.

Jim has written numerous curricula for business and leadership seminars, as well as many essays and articles. In addition to the PASSIONATE LIVES AND LEADERS series, he is the author of five other landmark books on leadership and organizational development:

- High-Performance Ethics: *10 Timeless Principles for Next Generation Leadership*
- Broaden the Vision and Narrow the Focus: *Managing in a World of Paradox*
- The Passionate Organization: *Igniting the Fire of Employee Commitment*
- Balance of Power: *Fueling Employee Power without Relinquishing Your Own*
- Fatal Illusions: *Shredding a Dozen Unrealities That Can Keep Your Organization from Success*

Prior to founding Luman International, Jim was President of EMCI, a high-tech design and manufacturer of aerospace systems and medical devices. Before that, he held managerial and executive positions at Hallmark Cards, VF Corporation, and Black & Veatch Consulting Engineers.

Jim is an award-winning senior faculty member of the American Management Association, where he served for several years as a charter member of the Faculty Advisory Council. He taught its premier course, The Course for Presidents (in which he was and is the highest-rated faculty member), and is the overall highest-rated faculty member in the history of the AMA. He is also a frequent presenter at the Center for Leadership & Executive Development. Jim has an extensive speaking schedule, in which he addresses topics from his books and research, and has been interviewed frequently on radio and television.

Jim received his education in leadership, business, economics, and engineering at the University of Missouri (Columbia and Rolla), where he received his Ph.D. (h.c.). He has also taught at Rockhurst University. Jim is past president of the Academy of Engineering Management, a member of the American Society for Training and Development, a member of the American Society of Engineering Management, a senior member of the Society of Manufacturing Engineers, and a registered professional engineer in Missouri and Kansas.

Jim has been honored with continuous listings in *Who's Who in America* (1999-2009), *Who's Who in the World* (1989-2008), and *Who's Who in Finance & Industry* (1989-2009).

PHIL HOTSENPILLER

Phil Hotsenpiller is an executive coach who brings his wealth of professional experience, creativity, and spiritual insight to passionate leaders around the world.

Phil is the founder and President of New York Executive Coaching Group, a firm that has assisted Presidents, CEOs, and other professionals to achieve breakthrough results in their professional and personal lives. His clients are a diverse and accomplished array of leaders in many sectors: arts and entertainment, finance and industry, and religious and not-for-profit.

Phil is also the Executive Director of the not-for-profit International Freedom (IF). IF is working with its partners to build 200 education centers for Dalit children and 200 vocational training centers for Dalit women throughout India. Using the power of documentary film, International Freedom also seeks to raise awareness among Hollywood "influencers" of the plight of the Dalit people in order to bring about lasting change. IF's acclaimed documentary, DELETES, was selected to compete in the Artivist Film Festival and the HollyShorts Film Festival, where it earned the Audience Choice Award. In addition, IF has recruited more than 1000 volunteers to serve urban Los Angeles, feeding the homeless and creating after-school programs and health clinics.

Throughout his career, Phil has worked extensively on issues at the nexus of leadership, artistry, and spirituality. Previously, he served as adjunct professor in a division of Southern Theological Seminary and Union Theological Seminary. He has spoken on leadership and theology throughout Mexico, Brazil, Paraguay, El Salvador, Honduras, Guatemala, Romania, Yugoslavia, and France, working with the European Team of Christian Associates International in the area of leadership development. He was one of 25 selected to serve on the Pastors Task Force for the War on Drugs organized by former U.S. "drug czar" William Bennett. Phil also founded *One Purpose*, a weekly television show on WSFJ-TV and a daily radio broadcast on WRFD radio.

Phil continues to address these issues, facilitating a weekly group of 100 prominent actors and young leaders in the Hollywood entertainment industry. With bestselling graphic novel artist/illustrator Rob Liefield, Phil is a founding partner of 12 Gates Productions, an entertainment company producing a full line of graphic novels, lithographs, DVDs, feature-length films, and video games. He currently serves as Teaching Pastor at Yorba Linda Friends Church in Southern California; YLFC was recently honored as one of the 100-fastest growing churches in the United States. As a leader of discovery trips to Europe, Phil teaches European history, art, philosophy, religion, and culture in Geneva, Amsterdam, and Aix-en-Provence. These trips provide participants with an understanding of different cultures and build bridges between passionate people around the world.

Phil received his education in history, religion, political science, and English literature at Southwest Baptist University. He earned his Master of Divinity from New Orleans Baptist Theological Seminary and completed postgraduate studies at Christ Church College, Oxford University.

Phil is married to Tammy Hotsenpiller, author of *A Taste of Humanity* (2009) and co-founder and designer of Humanity™ for All, LLC, a cutting-edge clothing line noted for its original art with an urban flair and its strong links with dozens of social justice organizations. Songwriter Tye-V (Nycolia Turman) is writing lyrics for an upcoming Humanity™ album.

THE PASSIONATE LIVES & LEADERS SERIES

Book 1 - The Passion Principle: *Designing a Passionate Organization*
Book 2 - The Attraction Principle: *Finding, Keeping and Teaming Passionate People*
Book 3 - The Thinking Principle: *Using Passion to Innovate and Create Value*
Book 4 - The Paradox Principle: *How Passionate Leaders Merge Competing Ideas*
Book 5 - The Performance Principle: *Delivering Results through the Power of Passion*
Book 6 - The Confidence Principle: *Discovering Your Life's Passion and a Place to Live It*
Book 7 - The Reality Principle: *Exploiting Change and Crisis with Courage and Passion*
Book 8 - The Influence Principle: *Communicating and Coaching to Ignite Passion*

You and every member of your organization will be inspired by this 8-book series in which real-world leaders share their experiences in building passionate teams and organizations. Read how the ultimate competitive advantage is harnessing the passion that leads to outstanding performance!

For more about THE PASSIONATE LIVES AND LEADERS SERIES, visit www.livesandleaders.com.

To order, or to learn more about volume discounts for individual books and sets, visit Quintessential Books at www.quintessentialbooks.com.

To learn more about implementing these principles, visit Luman International at www.lumaninternational.com

Quintessential Books

READ BOLDLY. THINK DEEPLY. LIVE PASSIONATELY.
www.quintessentialbooks.com